*The
Connell Guide
to*

The Rise and Fall of the Third Reich

---

by Caroline Sharples

Contents

Introduction	4
Germany before Hitler	
What was the impact of the First World War on Germany?	9
Why did the Weimar democracy fail?	15
The rise of the Nazis	
What was National Socialism?	23
How did Hitler gain power?	30
Who voted for Hitler?	37
The consolidation of power	
How did Hitler establish his dictatorship?	42
Was Hitler a weak dictator?	50
Life in the Third Reich	
How successful was Nazi domestic policy?	65
How widespread was German resistance to Hitler?	77
Foreign policy	
Did Hitler plan to go to war?	86

Racial policy

How did "ordinary" Germans respond to the persecution of the Jews?   94

When was the decision for the "Final Solution" taken?   102

Downfall

How did the Third Reich collapse?   110

NOTES

The German Reichs	*6*
Pre-war Germany	*14*
Adolf Hitler: a brief biography	*28*
The day of Potsdam	*48*
Leading Nazis	*56*
Ten facts about the Third Reich	*62*
The "Cult of the Führer"	*66*
The Volksgemeinschaft	*75*
The Terror State	*84*
The Nazi–Soviet Pact	*89*
Victims of Nazism	*94*
Glossary of Key Terms, Institutions and Abbreviations	*115*
A short chronology	*118*
Further reading	*123*

Introduction

Between 1933 and 1945, Germany was under the grip of the Third Reich. Headed by Adolf Hitler, this National Socialist state endeavoured to control every aspect of the nation's political, social, economic, religious and cultural life, and indoctrinate every German citizen in its ideology. The aim was to enact a thorough social revolution, eradicating both "weak" democratic institutions and old class divisions in order to establish a new "People's Community" constituted upon common blood ties. This intrinsically racist regime also embarked upon an expansionist foreign policy that, at its peak, brought most of continental Europe under Nazi control. The resulting war – and genocide – killed millions of soldiers and civilians and its effects continue to be felt to this day.

Nazism was not the only fascist movement to emerge in interwar Europe, but it harbours a unique, public fascination due to its peculiar racial character and levels of violence. Likewise, while the Holocaust was neither the first, nor the last, example of mass atrocity to take place in Europe, it was unprecedented in terms of its transnational reach and its industrial-scale killing methods, with purpose-built extermination centres constructed in occupied Poland. It was the Holocaust that bequeathed us the legal definition of "genocide" and "crimes against humanity" and the model for an international criminal court.

Furthermore, it is the Holocaust that stands at the forefront of contemporary genocide research, education and commemoration. These days, we have an international day of remembrance for the victims of Nazism, plus countless Holocaust memorials all over the world. Many countries have made studying the Third Reich a compulsory element of their school history curricula, offering a clear-cut morality tale for future generations about the dangers of racial intolerance. As historian Richard Evans has suggested, it is Nazism that is perceived as "the ultimate embodiment of evil".[*]

More than 70 years on, the Third Reich also continues to generate intense scholarly interest. There are continued questions about the roots of National Socialism, the workings of the Nazi state, the particular role of Hitler, the extent of popular support for Nazism, and the origins of both the Second World War and the Holocaust. In short, ever since 1945, historians have been grappling with one fundamental question: how was any of this possible in a modern, cultured nation at the heart of 20th century Europe?

The earliest accounts, based upon the documentary evidence submitted for the prosecution at the post-war Nuremberg trials, concentrated firmly on the Nazi leadership, state processes and key diplomatic events. By the 1970s, the wider development of social history saw this top-down

---

[*] Richard Evans, "Why are we so obsessed with the Nazis?", *The Guardian* (6 February 2015).

approach give way to new interest in *Alltagsgeschichte*, the history of everyday life under Nazism. Regional case studies began to flourish, along with investigations into the experiences of key social groups such as women and workers. Consequently, our understanding of the impact of Nazism started to become more nuanced, and scholars were able to engage in more in-depth studies of popular consensus and resistance.

Meanwhile, a revival of war crimes trials, especially that of former SS bureaucrat Adolf Eichmann in Jerusalem in 1961, helped to generate a new, critical investigation into the persecution of so-called "racial enemies". Historians began to make greater use of survivor testimonies and the

THE GERMAN REICHS

The literal translation of the term "Reich" is "realm", but has typically been used to denote a particular empire across three distinct periods of German history.

The first of these was the Heiliges Römisches Reich – the Holy Roman Empire which lasted from the Middle Ages to the Napoleonic Wars of the early 19th century. This stretched across central Europe including the areas that make up modern-day Germany, the Czech Republic and Northern Italy.

Later, the Deutsches Reich (literally, German Realm), also known as the Deutsches Kaiserreich (German Empire), was established in 1871 with the unification of Germany under Wilhelm I of Prussia; prior to this, the area we know today as Germany was actually a proliferation of numerous kingdoms, principalities and

very term "Holocaust" started to gain currency. Studies were undertaken into the complicity of key German institutions including the army, big business, the medical profession and the churches, and, by the 1990s, historians such as Daniel Goldhagen and Christopher Browning were engaging in a lively debate about the involvement of "ordinary Germans" in the crimes of the Third Reich. Today, there still remain numerous avenues for original research, with scholars tackling everything from the German public's knowledge of the pre-war concentration camps to cultural life under the Nazi regime.

As this volume will illustrate, much of the literature has crystallised around the so-called duchies. Technically, this "Deutsches Reich" persisted even after Germany's defeat in the First World War and the abdication of Wilhelm II (grandson of the original emperor).

The Nazis, though, refused to describe the Weimar period of 1918-1933 in these terms, denouncing the Republic as "un-German" and arguing that there had been a devastating break with the nation's noble history. Consequently, the period of Nazi rule from 1933 to 1945 was deliberately styled as the Drittes Reich (Third Reich). It was a title indicative of the Nazis' sense of nostalgia for a lost past, and fuelled the recurring motif of Hitler being the latest in a long line of strong, heroic German leaders, someone who could restore the country's fortunes. That is why the Nazi regime continues to be labelled as the Third Reich. But while the Nazis would have described the earlier realms as the "First" and "Second" Reichs, historians generally prefer to avoid these terms, being understandably unwilling to perpetuate the Nazi vision of history. ∎

Intentionalist-Structuralist debate. The former school of thought, typified by the likes of Karl-Dietrich Bracher, Eberhard Jäckel and Lucy Dawidowicz, emphasises the totalitarian nature of Nazi Germany, presenting Hitler as the omnipotent leader who possessed a consistent set of ideological goals and a clear programme for implementing them. The latter group of scholars, typified by Hans Mommsen and Martin Broszat, rejects this, arguing that the structure of the Third Reich was fundamentally confused, with ad hoc decision-making and intense power rivalries generating a "cumulative radicalism" that eventually brought the entire regime tumbling down. A third way, posited by Ian Kershaw in the early 1990s, fuses elements of both the Intentionalist and Structuralist arguments, acknowledging the inherent confusion within the Nazi state, but still presenting Hitler as the ultimate source of authority.

As these competing theories show, there is no easy way to sum up the Third Reich but therein lies its enduring fascination. It is a period of history that shocks and appals us, but also challenges our thinking about human behaviour. Consequently, the rise and fall of the Nazi regime will continue to occupy our historical consciousness for many years to come.

Germany before Hitler

What was the impact of the First World War on Germany?

When war was declared in August 1914, it was greeted with great public enthusiasm. Across the country, large crowds gathered to cheer the news, generating a display of national unity that would become much mythologised amid the political and economic instability of the post-war years. As Germans rushed to the colours, there was widespread belief that victory would soon be at hand.

In reality, of course, the First World War dragged on for another four years. Germany did enjoy notable success on the eastern front and made some early advances in the west, but the latter theatre of war soon developed into a stalemate. In 1916, the navy was humiliated at the Battle of Jutland and remained in harbour for the remainder of the conflict. Unrestricted submarine warfare had the primary effect of bringing the United States on to the opposite side of the war in 1917, while an Allied blockade of German ports resulted in desperate food and fuel shortages, declining public morale and political unrest. Hopes for a renewed offensive in spring 1918 proved costly and eventually, on 11 November 1918, the Armistice was signed. Negotiations for a peace settlement then began in Versailles in January 1919.

Most narratives of the Third Reich necessarily start with this earlier chapter of German history because it had such a profound impact on the country's political and economic landscape. Some two million German soldiers were killed in the conflict, creating a demographic imbalance. The post-war government would have to find the means to support the war-widowed and the war-disabled, while also contending with the rampant inflation caused by financing the war effort through a series of loans.

The notion that the country had been defeated in the First World War was unbelievable to many people, particularly since Allied troops had not even entered the country. Immediately, a myth sprang up that Germany had not lost the war in any military sense, but had been "stabbed in the back" by pernicious enemies at home. Most of the blame was attached to the Jews who were falsely accused of shirking their duty in the conflict. Such legends would endure throughout the interwar period, appropriated and exaggerated by the Nazi Party in propaganda that provided a convenient scapegoat for all of the nation's ills.

The post-war peace settlement produced even more bitterness. The German delegation was excluded from the negotiations at Versailles and merely handed a list of terms to sign. This immediately prompted accusations that the settlement was a

Diktat – a dictated peace and nothing more than an act of vengeance on the part of the victors. The terms themselves seemed devastating. Germany was stripped of her overseas colonies (which would now be administered by Britain and France), and lost swathes of territory on her east and west European borders. Alsace and Lorraine, annexed after the Franco-Prussian war in 1871, were restored to France, while the Rhineland that separated the two countries was to be demilitarised.

The industrially-rich Saarland was also to be administered by France for a period of 15 years. Elsewhere, northern Schleswig was given to Denmark, parts of Upper Silesia were given to the newly-formed Czechoslovakia and a "Polish corridor" was created between east and west Prussia. Danzig was to become a free city. Disarmament clauses, meanwhile, restricted the German army to 100,000 men and the navy to just six battleships. Submarines were prohibited, as was the use of an air force or conscription into the armed forces.

The most notorious part of the treaty, though, came with Article 231: the so-called "War Guilt" clause which attributed all of the responsibility for the conflict to German aggression. This, in turn, enabled the Allies to impose a hefty reparations bill on the Germans. But the notion that Germany should bear all the blame for the conflict rankled immediately with the German delegation at Versailles. Count Brockdorff-Rantzau was emphatic as he declared "such a confession would be…

a lie".* Back in Germany itself, crowds demonstrated in the Berlin Lustgarten while Prime Minister Philipp Scheidemann described the settlement as a "horrific and murderous witch's hammer".** A petition was sent to the Allies on 22 June 1919, arguing that the conditions proposed were beyond anything Germany could hope to achieve. The protest, however, went unheard and Germany was forced to sign the Treaty of Versailles on 28 June.

The outcome of the First World War would remain a popular grievance among the German people thereafter and, while various political parties campaigned on an anti-Versailles platform and a pledge to make Germany great again, it was the Nazis who proved most adept at channelling public outrage into mass support. In 1927, a still relatively unknown Adolf Hitler stressed the sheer propaganda potential that was bound up in this hated peace treaty, exclaiming that "this instrument of boundless blackmail and the most humiliating degradation could become the means... for the whipping up of national passions to boiling point!"***

Given the subsequent rise of Nazism, the Treaty of Versailles has been duly subjected to intense scholarly scrutiny over the years. Was it too harsh on Germany? Was it an inherently flawed compromise

---

* Count Brockdorff-Rantzau, 7 May 1919. Cited in R.F. Holt & A. Pickard (eds), *Democracy, Dictatorship, Destruction: Documents of Modern German History 1918-45* (Melbourne: Longman, 1991) p. 47.
** Philipp Scheidemann, 12 May 1919. Cited in Ibid, p. 49.
*** Adolf Hitler, 1927. Cited in Ibid, p. 52.

Adolf Hitler, Hermann Göring and Joseph Goebbels saluting during the singing of the Nazi anthem

between disparate Allied aims? Certainly, the Allies had gone into the peace talks with very different objectives. France, which had borne the brunt of the conflict, wanted to make Germany pay, literally in the form of reparations, and symbolically in the loss of territory and status. There was also a steely determination to ensure that Germany was so weakened that it could never again threaten France's borders. By contrast, the United States adopted a more moderate tone. President Woodrow Wilson had ambitions for an international disarmament agreement, freedom of the seas, the right for self-determination among national minorities and the creation of a League of Nations to safeguard world peace. Caught in between these two powers, Britain hoped to destroy German naval strength, while Italy simply wanted to gain more territory.

Against such a background, it was always going to be difficult to reach an agreement that satisfied everyone. Anthony Lentin suggests that the terms did not go far enough: Germany was weakened, but not so much that it could not wage war again; moreover, the sense of humiliation that the Treaty evoked would make Germany determined to undermine it wherever possible.* More recently, scholars such as Sally Marks, Ruth Henig and William Carr have argued that the fundamental problem lay not so much with the terms of the Treaty itself, but with the Allies' unwillingness to actually enforce it throughout the 1920s and 1930s.

* Anthony Lentin, *Guilt at Versailles* (Leicester: Methuen, 1984).

PRE-WAR GERMANY

At the start of the 20th century, Germany was ruled by Kaiser Wilhelm II, the grandson of Wilhelm I who had overseen the nation's belated unification back in 1871. The Kaiserreich, or Imperial Germany, as this period is generally known, had universal male suffrage and a parliament (the Reichstag) that housed various political parties. Yet this was also very much an authoritarian regime. Real power remained invested in the Emperor himself, and it was he who had the ability to appoint – or dismiss – his chancellor.

Within the political sphere, it was the rural, landowning elite that continued to wield the greatest influence, despite the fact that the majority of people now lived in cities.

Consequently, a socialist movement led by the Social

Yet however one interprets the peace settlement, it is too simplistic to draw a straight line from Versailles to Hitler's appointment as German chancellor in 1933. Many other factors came into play and the history of the post-war Weimar Republic itself needs to be considered if we are to understand how the Third Reich ever came about.

Why did the Weimar democracy fail?

On 9 November 1918, the Social Democratic politician Philipp Scheidemann stood at the window of the Reich Chancellery in Berlin and proclaimed a new political era for Germany. Kaiser Wilhelm II, who had ruled the country for 30 years, had abdicated, the monarchy was abolished

---

Democratic Party (SPD) had been developing during the late 19th century which called for political and social reforms. While these efforts were temporarily interrupted by the outbreak of the First World War, the ideas would not simply fade away. Instead, demands for revolutionary change would re-emerge from 1918 and characterise much of the interwar period.

Since 1888, Imperial Germany had been keen to flex its international muscles and find its own "place in the sun", pursuing overseas colonies in the Pacific and in Africa. Germany consequently came into direct competition with the older colonial powers, especially Britain and France. This, together with a developing arms race, heightened nationalism and a wave of popular militarism, all contributed to rising tensions that, ultimately, would spill over into the First World War as Germany and Austria-Hungary took on the combined weight of Britain, France and Russia. ∎

and a new republic was to be formed in its stead. The authoritarian style of rule that had characterised Germany since the nation's unification in 1871 was to be replaced by parliamentary democracy. This Weimar Republic subsequently drafted what was, at the time, one of the most advanced, liberal constitutions in Europe, with clauses guaranteeing freedom of speech, assembly and worship, universal suffrage and unfettered elections. Just 15 years later, though, all of this lay in tatters as Adolf Hitler stripped away people's civil rights and imposed his brutal dictatorship.

What went wrong? Historians have wrestled with this problem for many years, contemplating a wide array of both internal and external, short and long term factors that may have contributed to the Republic's demise. Most early studies focused predominantly on its final years, stressing the devastating impact of the 1929 Wall Street Crash and subsequent Great Depression that, at its peak, left six million Germans unemployed. Such accounts highlight the government's slow response to the crisis, its inability to cope with the sudden surge in welfare demands and, of course, the aptitude of extremist groups like Hitler's Nazi Party to exploit popular grievances in their propaganda. Even more significantly, it seems that by the start of the 1930s many Weimar politicians were simply unwilling to take measures to safeguard the fragile democracy. When push came to shove, most people harked back to the idea that having a single, strong leader was the best means of solving the nation's ills.

But is this enough to account for the abandonment of the Republic? Dissatisfied with the emphasis on short-term issues, a second wave of historians, writing in the late 1970s and early 1980s, switched their attention to the very origins of the Republic, asking whether, in fact, it had always been doomed to fail. As Richard Bessel sums up, "virtually the entire literature about the Weimar Republic has as its central theme the problem of its fundamental instability".[*]

Certainly, the fledgling Weimar Republic faced tremendous social, economic and political challenges from the off. First, there was a failure to enact a thorough revolution in 1918/19. Throughout the autumn of 1918, there had been growing public unrest about the state of the German war effort. This erupted into sailors' mutinies in the ports of Kiel and Wilhelmshaven, followed by the formation of workers' and soldiers' councils across Germany which, inspired by the success of the Russian Revolution the previous year, demanded a complete political change.

The new Republic was headed by the left-wing SPD but for some Germans things had not gone far enough. Bloody street fighting ensued and in January 1919 the Spartacist Uprising, headed by Rosa Luxembourg and Karl Liebknecht, called for

---

[*] Richard Bessel, *Social Change and Political Development in Weimar Germany* (London, 1981) p. 11.

a new, Soviet-style republic to be established.

Fearing this threat from the radical Left, the new Weimar chancellor, Friedrich Ebert, turned to the Freikorps, a right-wing group of ex-servicemen, to crush the revolt. An important precedent had been set: a pact with army officials enabled the Freikorps to remain free from government interference in return for providing protection for the new regime. Consequently, the old conservative elites were left in place, and there was no radical restructuring of German society. These people could simply bide their time and wait for an opportune moment to regain the initiative and restore Germany to its former way of life. The potential threat from the political right was underestimated as the government fixated on the fear of Bolshevism, while members of the political left were disillusioned as it became apparent that reform would remain limited. Further attempted coups would continue throughout the early 1920s.

Second, the new Weimar Republic was undermined by innate structural weaknesses. A system of proportional representation sounded fair on paper but, in reality, meant that no one party was able to gain a majority. A series of weak coalition governments fragmented the political system, hindered the passage of legislation and enabled extremist parties to gain a greater voice in the Reichstag during times of popular unrest. Meanwhile, Article 48 of the Weimar Constitution ensured that, in times of emergency, the President could pass decrees without going through the Reichstag. Just what would constitute an "emergency", though, was left open to interpretation. During the final years of the Republic, successive chancellors increasingly resorted to Article 48 as they struggled to contend with the economic crisis, steadily undermining democracy in the process. Most notoriously, it was Article 48 that would give Hitler the means to establish his rule in 1933.

Third, the Weimar Republic was weakened immediately by the economic legacy of the First World War. Even before the Treaty of Versailles had thrown reparations payments into the mix, the Germans were contending with vast amounts of debt and spiralling inflation. The situation was then exacerbated by the infamous 1919 peace treaty. Saddled with all the guilt for the First World War, Germany was compelled to pay billions of compensation to the Allies while at the same time being stripped of some of her most industrially-rich territories.

By 1923, the country was in the grip of hyperinflation, the currency was worthless and millions of people had lost their life savings. While the introduction of the Rentenmark enabled the economy to recover, the shadow of reparations continued to loom over the country for the rest of the interwar period. Two international agreements (the Dawes Plan of 1925 and the Young Plan of 1929) would revise the overall amount that Germany had to pay, and enable her to borrow the necessary funds from the United States. Yet the economic burdens imposed after the First World War remained extremely unpopular, providing powerful ammunition to right-wing groups who called for a complete rejection of the whole Versailles settlement. Reliance on US loans also left Germany especially vulnerable to further financial disaster when the Wall Street Crash struck in October 1929.

Fourth, the new republic simply lacked popular legitimacy. Liberal, parliamentary democracy was still a novelty for Germany at this time and many viewed it with suspicion. Some branded themselves as "republicans by reason" – they would go along with the new system while there was little viable alternative but they were not wholly convinced by it; their support was based on rational or strategic decision-making, rather than ideological conviction. Count Henry Kessler summed this up when describing the shambolic nature of Ebert's swearing-in ceremony as the first Weimar President in 1919. The event, he suggested, was "all very decorous, but lacking go"; that such a "petty drama" should follow after the "tremendous events of war and revolution" was frustrating and disappointing.[*] This begs the question: if the Republic could not capture hearts and minds in its earliest hours, how many people would really be prepared to fight for it when it was under attack by anti-democratic forces?

---

[*] Count Henry Kessler, 21 August 1919. Reproduced in A. Kaes, M. Jay & E. Dimendberg (eds), *The Weimar Republic Sourcebook* (Berkley, California: University of California Press, 1994) pp.51-2.

Even more significant was the Republic's unfortunate association with Germany's recent defeat in the First World War. The politicians who had signed the Armistice became known as the "November Criminals", guilty of treason. That some of these men were Jewish added further grist to the "stab in the back" rhetoric being peddled by the political right. This, combined with the fledgling government being forced to sign the hated Treaty of Versailles, ensured that the Republic's reputation was tainted from the start, and various political parties – not just the Nazis – spent the next few years campaigning to reverse the process and make Germany great again.

Ultimately, the Weimar Republic has to be recognised very much as a post-war society struggling to make the transition to peace after a bloody four year conflict that had left the nation psychologically scarred, demographically depleted, and economically weakened. It is possible to see a certain desensitisation to violence, with First World War veterans joining paramilitary groups and engaging in bloody skirmishes with political enemies. Popular militarism and aggressive nationalism persisted and, in broader popular culture, the majority of books and films continued to present war as a glorious and noble pursuit. For younger males, cheated of their own glittering military career by the post-war restrictions on the German army, joining the Hitler Youth or the *Sturmabteilung* (SA – the Nazi paramilitary group) became an important outlet for expression.

The "doomed to fail" narrative of Weimar Germany, though, can only get us so far in our understanding of the interwar period. The notion that a Hitler-type figure was somehow inevitable is too simplistic and fails to take into account the political choices that were available to Germans in the 1920s and early 1930s. Furthermore, there was even a period during the mid 1920s when the Republic looked as if it might yet survive. These so-called "golden years" between 1924 and 1928 were characterised by relative political and economic stability, Germany's rehabilitation on the international stage through membership of the League of Nations, and a vibrant, flourishing culture of modernity.

New technologies, rising consumer culture, and significant welfare reforms all help to justify a more positive assessment of the republic – yet these did not silence the reactionary voices. Some commentators critiqued the perceived loss of traditional family values as the so-called "New Woman" broke with gender norms and went out to work. Others bemoaned the "Americanisation" of German culture, and concerns were raised about flight from the land as more people, especially younger Germans, headed to the city for new opportunities. It is thus no coincidence that a promise of getting "back to basics" became part of the Nazis' campaign platform, idealising rural ways of living and reminiscing about a simpler time.

In short, there is no single factor that can be held up to explain the collapse of the Weimar Republic in 1933. Political disappointments, economic crisis, social stress and a general lack of passion for democracy combined to create a perfect storm that the Nazis could take advantage of.

The rise of the Nazis

What was National Socialism?

As the Nazi Party began to gain ground at the start of the 1930s, many German intellectuals were left wondering just what, if anything, the party was all about. In 1932, for instance, Fritz Gerlich argued that, "the leadership of the Hitler party has absolutely no convictions" beyond the simple seizure of power. Likewise, the novelist Thomas Mann described Nazism as "wishy-washy jargon", albeit jargon that was infused with "hatred", "barbarism" and "primitive popular vulgarity".[*] Historians, too, have long debated the nature of National Socialism. Should it be regarded as just another example of European fascism, or was there something different about this particular movement? Was it merely a reactionary protest party, or did it actually stand *for* something?

[*] Cited in Neil Gregor (ed.), *Nazism: A Reader* (Oxford: Oxford University Press).

The German Workers' Party was formed in Munich in 1919. Led by local railwayman Anton Drexler, it emerged out of the bitterness of defeat in the First World War and harboured a fervent belief in *völkisch* (ethno-)nationalism. The party was anti-marxist, anti-capitalist and antisemitic. In September 1919, an army intelligence agent named Adolf Hitler was ordered to report on one of the party's beer hall meetings. Far from remaining in an observatory role, Hitler was quickly drawn into a heated debate about the concept of a "Greater Germany". Dazzling Drexler with his own passionate rhetoric on the theme, he was immediately invited to join up. From then onwards, Hitler was an integral party member, intimately involved in organising propaganda and the drafting of the party programme, the so-called 25 Points published on 24 February 1920. That same day, the organisation changed its name to the National Socialist German Workers' Party (NSDAP) and, by 1921, Hitler had taken over as leader.

To understand National Socialism, we can do no better than to turn to the 25 points, one of the most extensive documents on Nazi ideology ever to be produced by the party. The programme, with its repetition of "we demand" in every point, revealed both a list of grievances and a desire to appeal to as many elements of the German population as possible. Examining it reveals several major themes.

The first three points were all about a rejection

of the hated Treaty of Versailles, calling for a "union of all Germans" (in other words, the forbidden union with Austria), the "abrogation" of the post-war peace settlement and for "land and territory" to sustain the German people. Collectively, these opening demands underscored the extent to which the Nazi party was a product of the First World War. As well as desiring the restoration of German strength, they also introduced the central concept of *Lebensraum* (living space) to sustain a growing population. This required German expansion, advances that would no doubt bring the country into conflict with other nations. With point 22 also calling for the restoration of the German army, these aggressive sentiments can be viewed as evidence that the Nazis were planning for war.

Point 4 of the Party Programme revealed the racism that was so intrinsic to Nazism. It stated simply: "only a member of the race can be a citizen. A member of the race can only be one who is of German blood... Consequently, no Jew can be a member of the race." The positioning of this statement so early on in the programme indicates the fundamental importance attached to this belief. Elsewhere, there were further references to race in points 5, 6, 7, 8 and 23. Collectively, these sections of the manifesto made it very clear that "non-citizens" (in other words, Jews) would be expelled from public office, banned from working for or owning German newspaper firms, and subject to possible expulsion from the Reich. At the same time, future immigration was to be prevented. This, then, was a party that believed in the presence of "racial enemies" and would take measures to strip certain minorities of their civil rights. Similar scapegoating and racial stereotypes were evident in the party's visual propaganda throughout the 1920s and early 1930s, so people could be in little doubt that a vote for the NSDAP was a vote for a rabidly antisemitic and discriminatory party.

Concerns for the racial health of the so-called "Aryan" population were also evident from the start. Point 21, for instance, stressed the need to improve the physical fitness of the German people, pledging physical instruction for younger citizens, as well as greater protection for mothers and young children. This, in turn, links into another crucial feature of Nazi ideology: the concept of the *Volksgemeinschaft*, or "People's Community" (points 10 and 25), based upon ethnicity. This utopian vision of society would see the eradication of former class divisions and all Germans treated as equals. Consequently, many of the NSDAP's other demands had socialist overtones, pledging "equal rights and obligations" (9), the abolition of unearned income (11), the confiscation of war profits (12), profit-sharing and a nationalisation of industries (13 and 14).

Elsewhere, the party also promised welfare provision in old age (15), land reforms (17) and a widening of educational opportunities (20). Possibly there was room here for voters to look beyond the negative features of National Socialism and focus on these more progressive policies yet, as had already been made apparent in point 4, such measures would only be available to those deemed "citizens". Jews and other minorities would be excluded from the Volksgemeinschaft and all its anticipated benefits. An "us" and "them" dichotomy was being repeatedly promulgated in Nazi messages.

Finally, the 25 points highlighted the totalitarian aspirations of the Nazi movement. Great emphasis was placed on establishing a "strong central power" that would have "unlimited" authority. The readiness to impose state censorship was shown in point 23 with the promise to remove "destructive" artistic influences and to suppress any publications deemed to be against the "general good" of the community. All of this amounted to an explicit attack on the democratic values enshrined in the Weimar constitution. Elsewhere, point 18 provided an early threat of state terror, warning that "criminals", "usurers" and "profiteers" would be punished with the death penalty.

Little of the Nazi programme was actually original. Völkisch nationalism had been around since the early 19th century amid a resurgent interest in German folklore and tradition. Likewise, Pan-Germanism (the union of all German speaking peoples) had been a key element in debates as to whether a unified Germany should include Austria or not. The Jews, meanwhile, had already been subjected to centuries of persecution for their religious beliefs before pseudo-scientific theorists operating in the late 19th century began to talk of them as constituting a distinct *racial* group. Such ideas emerged amid a growing interest in eugenics and Social Darwinism, as well as a backlash against Jewish emancipation. National Socialism, however, took these existing ideas and breathed new life into them thanks to colourful propaganda, torchlight rallies and Hitler's own brand of fiery rhetoric. Nazism worked because it drew upon existing

ADOLF HITLER: A BRIEF BIOGRAPHY

Adolf Hitler was born on 20 April 1889 in Braunau am Inn on the Austrian-German border, a birthplace he would later describe as providential, given his dream of uniting these two German-speaking nations into a single Reich. He was the fourth of six children born to Alois Schickelgruber and Klara Hitler.

As a young man, Hitler dreamed of becoming a successful artist but was twice rejected from art school. Undeterred, he adopted a bohemian lifestyle in Vienna, struggling to forge a career painting watercolours. It was during this period that he developed his prejudice against Jews. By August 1914, he had moved to Munich where he greeted the outbreak of the First World War with immense enthusiasm, volunteering immediately for the Bavarian army.

During the conflict, Hitler showed bravery on several occasions, winning the Iron Cross First and Second Class. At the time of Germany's surrender in 1918, he was in hospital, having been temporarily blinded in a mustard gas attack and, like many Germans, news of the nation's defeat left him shocked and bitter.

stereotypes that people could understand and pulled together a mish-mash of promises that would attract a mass audience.

Thirteen years before Hitler became chancellor of Germany, the founding document of the NSDAP had already made clear that this was a divisive, racist, exclusionary, anti-democratic, aggressive, intolerant political movement. The themes set out in this programme would remain the central tenets of National Socialism, shaping the domestic and foreign policy of the Third Reich.

After the war, Hitler returned to Munich and served as an army intelligence agent, charged with gathering information on various fringe political movements. It was in this guise that he was, fatefully, introduced to the German Workers' Party in September 1919. Having assumed the role of leader of the party by 1921, he set about casting the party in his own image and embarked on his campaign for power, quickly becoming renowned for his ability as a passionate public speaker.

In 1932 Hitler ran, unsuccessfully, against Hindenburg for the presidency of the Weimar Republic, but this only served to galvanise his political ambitions. On 30 January 1933, he was handed the chancellorship and, a year later, became the sole leader of Germany following the death of Hindenburg. He continued to rule the country for the next 12 years.

Hitler was vegetarian and teetotal but rumours have long abounded about his physical and mental health. While definitive proof of his medical conditions is hard to come by, it does seem that he was suffering from Parkinson's and taking a range of prescription drugs by the end of his life. As Soviet forces advanced on Berlin in April 1945, he finally married his long-term companion Eva Braun and the pair committed suicide. He was 55 when he died. ■

How did Hitler gain power?

On 30 January 1933, Adolf Hitler was named as Germany's new chancellor. Shortly afterwards, the Nazis were talking proudly of a *Machtergreifung* – a seizure of power. Such rhetoric fitted perfectly with the NSDAP's self-image as the party of decisive action, but it was just rhetoric. In reality, the Nazis' efforts to gain power had passed through three distinct phases: an effort to grab control by force; the democratic pursuit of votes through the electoral process; and a period of intense political intrigue, playing other politicians and interest groups off against one another. Looking at each step of this process enables us to question the inevitability of Hitler's appointment as chancellor and examine how the NSDAP managed to hone its techniques to attract greater support.

Hitler's first attempt to grab power came with the Munich Putsch of 8-9 November 1923. It was a time of significant economic crisis for Germany. Hyperinflation was rampant and, with the country having recently defaulted on a reparations payment, the Ruhr had been occupied by French and Belgian forces. This prompted an outpouring of nationalism in Germany and was fertile material for right-wing groups wishing to overthrow Weimar democracy. The Nazis, emboldened by the fact that Bavaria was already a hotbed for the political right, believed that they could count on the firm support of the local police and army. The fact that Mussolini had gained power in Italy after his march in Rome[*] was no doubt another cause for encouragement. Finally, the precise timing of this putsch was significant: 9 November 1923 marked the fifth anniversary of the proclamation of the Weimar Republic so this would be a clear symbol of anti-democratic forces taking back control.

Accordingly, on 8 November, the Nazis raided a beer hall meeting of Bavarian government officials and declared the beginnings of a national uprising. The local political leaders and army officers were pressured into joining the planned march to take over the national government but, overnight, these men reneged on their promise. The next day, police barricades were erected and additional armed troops were brought in to suppress the revolt. Without the promised support of the army leadership, the Nazis' putsch collapsed, though not before 16 party members had been killed in a gun battle with police. In the aftermath, Hitler was arrested for high treason.

On the surface, the Munich Putsch was a complete failure yet it would have important repercussions. Hitler's trial gave him a platform to extol his ideology to a much wider audience, and he wasted little time in portraying himself as a loyal patriot who only wanted what was best for Germany. He certainly won over the court, coming away with

---

* The so-called March on Rome, involving between 20,000 and 30,000 people, took place between October 22 and 29 1922, and led to Mussolini's fascist party taking over the government.

a lenient sentence of five years' imprisonment. Just nine months of this were actually served, during which time Hitler dictated what would become the central text for the National Socialist movement, *Mein Kampf*. Most significantly, though, the events of 1923 prompted a fundamental change in tactics. From here on, the NSDAP would participate in elections and seek power through the ballot box.

The Nazi decision to resort to democratic methods, however, should not be taken as any indicator of a change in attitude to the Weimar Republic. As Joseph Goebbels made abundantly clear in a 1928 edition of the party newspaper, the Nazis did not intend to enter the Reichstag to prop it up. "We do not want to join this pile of manure," he stressed, "we are coming to shovel it out."[*]

Upon Hitler's release, the NSDAP duly set about reorganising themselves, honing their propaganda message and tailoring it carefully to appeal to as many social groups as possible. Initially, the relative peace and prosperity of the mid 1920s ensured that the NSDAP remained a fringe movement. In the May 1928 Reichstag elections, for example, the party polled just 2.6 per cent of the national vote, with the majority of support coming from their Franconian heartland. It was not until September 1930 that the Nazis made their national breakthrough, capturing just over 18 per cent of the vote and 107 seats in the Reichstag. The timing

---

[*] Joseph Goebbels, "Why do we want to join the Reichstag?", *Der Angriff*, 30 April 1928.

Soldiers in a regimental band goose-stepping in a military parade in honour of Hitler's 50th birthday

owes much to the impact of the Great Depression. The Wall Street stock market had crashed in October 1929 and Germany, reliant on US loans to fund its reparations payments, had been especially hard hit. As the economic crisis worsened, the population began to turn to the extremist parties with both the NSDAP and the KPD seeing big gains. By July 1932, the NSDAP was polling 37.3 per cent of the vote, becoming the largest political party in the Reichstag with 230 seats.

Propaganda, and in particular the representation of Hitler, was a crucial factor behind this swell in popular support. As unemployment crept up to six million, the NSDAP campaigned on a simple message of providing "bread and work" to the people. Desperate times, it was argued, called for strong, decisive leadership – something that seemed all too lacking from the succession of coalition governments that came and went during the early 1930s. Most NSDAP posters drew upon the image of the strong German worker who would rebuild the nation's prospects, while the party symbol of the swastika was frequently presented rising like a sun on the horizon, promising a "new dawn" for Germany. Hitler himself was depicted as a messianic figure bathed in heavenly light and leading the country forwards towards victory.

The eye-catching posters with their vivid use of colour were accompanied by other, more novel forms of propaganda, including torchlight processions and mass rallies. These served to capture the public imagination and make the NSDAP stand out from traditional parties. Similarly, during his 1932 bid for the presidency, Hitler flew all over the country to meet as many voters as possible. This "Hitler over Germany" campaign was documented in the nation's newsreel footage and the NSDAP even published a commemorative booklet of photographs from this unprecedented tour. The message was clear: this was a politician who would not simply sit behind a desk, but one who would actually get things done.

At the same time, the NSDAP proved adept at offering the public a clear set of scapegoats who could be blamed for all of Germany's problems. The Jew was repeatedly singled out in campaign propaganda as the primary "enemy" of the nation, variously depicted as a grotesque, satanic caricature, or as a dangerous snake. Bolshevism and freemasonry were likewise vilified, alongside frequent attacks on Republican politicians. Germany, it was claimed, was being corroded by all of these pernicious forces and only Nazism possessed the strength and determination to eradicate them.

Flush with victory in the July 1932 elections, Hitler then set about trying to secure the position of chancellor for himself, but President Hindenburg, wary of the violence being unleashed by the SA, refused his request. While the Nazis may have won the most votes at the recent elections, they still lacked an overall majority so were in no real position to dictate terms. Undeterred, Hitler entered the third and final stage of his pursuit of power: a careful series of political manoeuvres that enabled him to play political rivals off against one another and gather the necessary backing to launch another bid at the chancellorship.

Between 1929 and 1933, Weimar Germany went through four different chancellors, but each one proved unable to grapple with the severity of the Great Depression or the immense strain now being placed upon the welfare state. Each government failed to capture support from the public and from the Reichstag, prompting a growing reliance on Article 48 to get legislation passed. Hitler, meanwhile, was busy cosying up to other conservative politicians, business leaders and representatives of the German army, pressing his case and telling each group how he would protect their interests. In the end, these people persuaded Hindenburg that appointing Hitler was the best means of avoiding civil war or a Communist takeover, and uttered assurances that he could be safely controlled; they would be using his popularity with the masses but real political power would still rest with the traditional conservatives.

Such claims were based upon the constituency of Hitler's first cabinet which would include just three Nazis (including Hitler himself) and the fact that Franz von Papen, the former chancellor, would serve as vice chancellor, ensuring a steadying hand in the new government. Yet such precautions proved short-sighted. The conservative elites overlooked Hitler's ruthless ambition to become sole ruler of Germany, as well as the fact that the other two Nazis in the cabinet had not been given just any old jobs, but positions that could enable them to play a serious role in dismantling the democratic organs of the Weimar Republic. Wilhelm Frick, as Minister of the Interior, wielded control over the police and domestic security while Hermann Göring held the equivalent post for Prussia, the largest German state.

In the final analysis, it cannot be said that Hitler "seized" power in 1933, nor was he voted directly into office. Instead, he had the chancellorship handed to him on a plate after a series of political intrigues and miscalculations, and he would waste little time in advancing his cause even further.

Who voted for Hitler?

By July 1932, the NSDAP had grown from a small movement on the lunatic fringe of German politics to become the largest single party in the Reichstag. Its share of the vote had jumped 35 per cent in just four years, but where was this surge in popular support coming from?

Trying to piece together the constituency of the Nazi vote has proved a challenging process for historians given the fragmentary nature of the surviving evidence. What is clear, though, is that outside the party's heartland in Franconia, some of the strongest, earliest support actually came from northern parts of the country. In 1924, for example, the percentage of NSDAP support was 8.6 per cent in East Prussia and nearly 21 per cent in Mecklenburg, compared with a national average of 6.5 per cent. The reasons behind this lay with the particular social, economic and confessional characteristics of these districts. Both East Prussia and Mecklenburg were predominantly rural areas facing a growing agricultural crisis. Rising debts, falling agricultural prices, an export crisis and a growing number of farm foreclosures all contributed to public grievances here.

The Nazis were quick to alter their campaign strategy to exploit all this, realising that an investment in propaganda in these more remote regions yielded better returns than the large urban centres where there was increased competition from rival political parties. A wave of propaganda presenting the peasant farmer as the "backbone" of the German nation and the ideal, physically fit specimen of the "Aryan" race no doubt had a flattering effect too. By contrast, urban centres tended to resist the allure of National Socialism for longer. The SPD and KPD (the German communist party) were more entrenched here and were particularly able to draw upon the support of manual labourers. Düsseldorf East, for example, remained the last bastion of anti-Nazi parties up to 1933.

The regions polling the greatest support for the NSDAP were also predominantly Protestant. The Church tolerated or shared in a lot of Nazi ideology, and welcomed the party's promise to effect a return to "positive Christianity". And there was no single, identifiably "Protestant" political party to dominate this share of the vote. By contrast, regions containing a higher concentration of Catholics, such as the Rhineland and parts of southern Germany, displayed a steady loyalty to the Catholic Centre party throughout this period. There were, of course, some exceptions to these trends. Dick Geary points out that towns like Breslau and Legnitz saw significant Nazi support, despite being in a traditionally Catholic region. Here, though, it seems that local racial tensions between Germans and Poles played a part in influencing voting behaviour.*

In terms of class, the core Nazi support is generally recognised as having come from the so-called *Mittelstand* – the lower middle class made up of small businessmen, artisans and peasant farmers. These groups clung to the traditional social hierarchy and were wary of the growing threat from both trade unionism and big business. Increased government interference and high taxation had added to their list of grievances. Here, the NSDAP's anti-Bolshevik, anti-capitalist and anti-democratic message held particular appeal and it was these lower middle class elements that came to be over-represented within the NSDAP membership itself.

The role of other social groups has generated rather more scholarly debate. Traditionally, it was assumed that, despite the Hitler movement positioning themselves as the National Socialist German *Workers'* Party, the working class remained immune to Nazi propaganda, backing the SPD or KPD instead. More recent research, though, reveals that the Nazis did, in fact, make significant gains in working class districts like Saxony. Furthermore, closer analysis of the available statistics has shown that 55 per cent of SA members and 40 per cent of NSDAP membership stemmed from people of working class origins. Many of these came from areas lacking a strong SPD presence.

* Dick Geary, "Who voted for the Nazis?", *History Today*, Vol. 48, No. 10 (October 1998).

The response of white collar workers, meanwhile, was also more diverse than initially realised. Those in middle management positions were more likely to vote Nazi than those immediately below them yet those who originated from large cities or manual labouring backgrounds still tended to lean towards the SPD. As the economic crisis worsened, the political climate shifted. There is evidence that upper middle class voters from some of the wealthiest cities, including Berlin and Hamburg, switched their allegiance to the NSDAP at this time. Elsewhere, leading industrialists tended to hedge their bets, donating to several different parties in an effort to safeguard their interests.

Conventionally, Nazi support is explained in terms of the rising unemployment triggered by the Great Depression. Certainly, the party's electoral fortunes would seem to tie in to the unemployment statistics with both peaking in the summer of 1932. However, this is not the whole story. Most of those who joined the NSDAP had jobs, while the Nazi share of the vote was actually lower in cities with high levels of unemployment. Here, it was the communist KPD which was reaping the rewards of the economic crisis. Likewise, Nazism is frequently depicted as having particular appeal to German youth, not least since Hitler called directly for the younger generation to join with him. The majority of party members before 1930 fell into the 21-40 year old age group, yet the Nazis also managed to attract significant support among the elderly, a group wooed through Nazi promises to protect pensions and provide greater support for war veterans. This further complicates our image of the "typical" Nazi supporter.

Overall, it is fair to describe the NSDAP as a true party of the masses, managing to win votes and members from a wide cross-section of society, regardless of age and gender. This support, though, was concentrated in some regions more than others. People who had stronger existing political ties, lived in large towns, were Catholic or were unemployed were less inclined to support Nazism than their rural, Protestant counterparts. Once in power, though, the Nazis would be doing everything they could to win over all hearts and minds, drawing upon a combination of financial and social incentives, and threats of terror.

NAZI ELECTORAL SUPPORT: 1924–1933

Reichstag elections						
May 24	Dec. 24	May 28	Sept. 30	July 32	Nov. 32	Mar. 33
No. of seats						
32	14	12	107	230	196	288
% of national vote						
6.5	3.0	2.6	18.3	37.3	33.1	43.9

Table adapted from J. Noakes & G. Pridham (eds), *Nazism: A Documentary Reader 1919-1945. Vol. 1: The Rise to Power, 1919-1934* (Exeter: Exeter University Press, 1984). ■

The consolidation of power

How did Hitler establish his dictatorship?

Adolf Hitler may have become chancellor of Germany at the end of January 1933, but his overall power was still limited. There was no NSDAP majority in the Reichstag (the party's share of the vote had actually *declined* in the last round of elections in November 1932), and supreme authority continued to rest with the Weimar president, Paul von Hindenburg. Other crucial checks on Nazi power included the army, the civil service, rival political parties and, for what it was worth, public opinion. The challenge for Hitler was to find a way of uniting all of these groups under his control, a process known as *Gleichschaltung* (coordination). Part of this was achieved legally, cynically turning the Republic's democratic process against itself; the remainder was achieved through a combination of violence, intimidation and murder.

One of Hitler's first acts as chancellor was to call for a new election to be held on 5 March 1933. The hope was that this would finally give him the seats necessary to avoid further coalition governments. However, on 27 February 1933, the Reichstag itself went up in flames. With the new election less than a week away, the fire was seen as an attack on democratic values and clear evidence that there was a dangerous enemy at work in Germany. When a young Dutch communist, Marinus van der Lubbe, was arrested at the scene, the whole event was immediately blamed on the KPD.

Touring the charred wreckage for himself, Hitler expressed his righteous indignation at this wanton attempt to destroy the home of German politics, declaring; "there will be no mercy now. Anyone who stands in our way will be cut down."[*] The timing of the fire could not have been more convenient for the Nazis, to the extent that some conspiracists believe that it was the NSDAP itself that set the blaze. The consensus among historians, however, is that van der Lubbe was responsible and that the event was just a stroke of luck for the Nazis.

Whatever the exact cause of the fire, one thing is clear: it provided the crucial spark for the Nazis to move against their political opponents and start dismantling Weimar democracy. The very next day, the "Reichstag Fire Decree" was passed, suspending people's constitutional rights to free assembly, freedom of expression and a free press. The state was granted the authority to access mail and telephone conversations, search houses, confiscate property and hold people without trial. Although billed as a temporary, emergency measure to root

---

[*] Account by Rudolf Diehls, Head of the Prussian Political Police. Reproduced by German History in Documents and Images, http://germanhistorydocs.ghi-dc.org/sub_document.cfm?document_id=1494

out those responsible for this heinous attack, these rights would not actually be restored while the Nazis remained in government. At a stroke, Hitler gained far-reaching powers to deal with anyone deemed a threat to his rule. The KPD, of course, bore the initial brunt of this decree with party offices ransacked and members arrested. One of the Nazis' main rivals in the upcoming elections was thus suppressed.

Although the 5 March elections failed to yield the Nazis' desired majority, Hitler remained undeterred. Plans were drawn up for an Enabling Act that would allow the Reich *cabinet* to enact legislation, including measures that deviated from the constitution. The Act was presented as a means out of the tiresome, weak coalitions that had stymied successive Weimar governments; in reality, of course, it would enable Hitler to bypass the Reichstag entirely – and thus his lack of a parliamentary majority would no longer restrict his ability to manoeuvre. To come into effect, it needed to pass a Reichstag vote with a two thirds majority. The KPD voice had already been silenced thanks to the Reichstag Fire Decree, while SA troops gathered around the building to intimidate other would-be opponents. The Catholic Centre party was lured over to siding with the NSDAP by a promise that religious freedoms would be protected in this new Hitler state.

On 24 March 1933, the Reichstag duly voted 444-94 in favour of the Act. Only the SPD had the

Hitler consulting a geographical survey map with his general staff including Heinrich Himmler (L) and Martin Bormann (R) in 1932

courage of its convictions to oppose the bill. Once again, Hitler had utilised democratic processes to subvert the values they were supposed to protect. Legislative power now rested with the Reich Cabinet – but this was headed by Hitler, and the actual number of cabinet meetings would decline sharply as the Third Reich went on. Goebbels summed up this new state of affairs in his diary:

> the Führer's authority is now completely in the ascendant in the Cabinet. There will be no more

voting. The Führer's personality decides.*

The Reichstag would become a mere sounding board for Hitler's speeches. Just weeks after his appointment as chancellor, Hitler had demolished the parliamentary process and was setting himself up as dictator. The sheer pace of change was astonishing; indeed, even Goebbels confessed "all this has been achieved much more quickly than we had dared to hope".** It was a process, though, facilitated by fear mongering, thuggery and the acquiescence of fellow politicians.

As Hitler increased his grip over national politics, the Nazis were also steadily taking over the police and local government. All too frequently, the SA would terrorise a neighbourhood, prompting the central government to declare that local authorities were unable to cope. A new Nazi leader would then be appointed to take control. On 31 March 1933, the state governments were dissolved and reconstituted in a manner that favoured the NSDAP representatives. In this way, the NSDAP expanded its reach across Germany.

At the same time, potential rivals were being squeezed out. On 22 March 1933, the first concentration camp was opened at Dachau to hold Communists and other political opponents. On 2

* Joseph Goebbels, 22 April 1933. Reproduced in J. Noakes & G. Pridham (eds), *Nazism: A Documentary Reader 1919-1945. Vol. 1: The Rise to Power, 1919-1934* (Exeter: Exeter University Press, 1984) p. 163.
** Ibid.

May 1933, a ban was issued on trade unions meaning that their leaders could face a similar fate and, from 14 July 1933, other political movements were forced to dissolve. Less than six months after assuming power, the NSDAP was declared the only legal political party in Germany.

The consolidation of power, however, was not solely about integrating Nazis into existing state frameworks or removing external opponents. Another important dimension of this process was the steps taken to ensure that Hitler remained the pre-eminent figure within the National Socialist movement, and by the summer of 1934 there was growing concern about the influence of the SA. Since Hitler's accession to the chancellorship, this paramilitary group had been engaging in public acts of violence as they sought to carry through the rest of the Nazi revolution all at once. Hindenburg and other conservatives were concerned about the impact all this would have on the fragile economy, as well as on Germany's reputation abroad. The army leadership was similarly unhappy with the SA's stated ambition to become Germany's new fighting force. Hitler was compelled to remind the SA that the "national uprising" would be guided from above, and that they needed to be patient.

Words alone, though, could not contain the SA and thus, on 30 June 1934, the Nazi leadership resorted to more drastic measures with the "Night of the Long Knives". A bloody purge left at least 80 SA men dead, including the SA leader, Ernst Röhm.

At the same time, Hitler took the opportunity to eliminate some of his older party rivals, including Gregor Strasser, who had long been the voice for the "socialist" wing of the NSDAP and sought to take the Party in a different direction.

The event demonstrated that the regime was fully prepared to use terror tactics to get what it wanted. The remaining SA forces were brought firmly to heel while the *Schutzstaffel* (Protection Squadron – the SS) that had carried out the purge emerged as the pre-eminent paramilitary organisation in the Third Reich. With Hitler choosing army interests over his own SA troops, he also secured himself the support of a powerful interest group

THE DAY OF POTSDAM

One of the most iconic steps in Hitler's consolidation of power came on 21 March 1933: the Day of Potsdam. The Nazis took a traditional ceremony marking the opening of a new Reichstag session and transformed it into an elaborate propaganda spectacle. The event was loaded with symbolism.

First, it was moved from its usual venue in Berlin to the Garrison Church in the nearby city of Potsdam where the remains of Frederick the Great, and other great military heroes of Germany, were buried. In a flash, Hitler was presenting himself as one of a long line of strong leaders and underscoring his own legitimacy to rule.

Second, the date for the institution of the new Reichstag was also shifted to coincide with the first day of spring – another powerful metaphor for the nation's rejuvenation under the new National Socialist government.

Third, the event witnessed a historic handshake between

that was crucial not only for implementing his foreign policy ambitions but for safeguarding himself against a potential military coup.

Finally, on 2 August 1934, the ailing President Hindenburg died, aged 86. Hitler used his Enabling Act to pass the "Law Concerning the Highest State Office of the Reich", fusing the posts of chancellor and president to leave himself as the supreme ruler (*Führer*) of Germany. The army swore an oath of loyalty to Hitler personally and the Nazi takeover of power was complete. From this point on, Germany was under a Hitler dictatorship.

---

the ageing President Hindenburg and his new chancellor which personified the sense of the "old" and the "new" Germany coming together and a restoration of national unity after so many years of political and economic upheaval.

Hitler, dressed in civilian clothes, bowed humbly before the head of state and cut a respectful figure. This stood in stark contrast to his prior image as a belligerent, fascist, rabble-rousing leader of a party perhaps best known for its beer-hall brawls, and was designed to reassure.

It was especially significant since it was occurring just three days before the vote on the Enabling Act that would give Hitler's cabinet full legislative powers. The course of the ceremony was relayed over loudspeaker and on the radio to reach as large an audience as possible.

Additional parades were staged in other cities across the country while the evening was marked by torchlight processions. The Day of Potsdam demonstrated the Nazis' gift for putting on impressive public displays and showed how Hitler could adapt his image to appease potential critics and get what he wanted. ■

Was Hitler a weak dictator?

From August 1934, Germany was a one party state under the control of Adolf Hitler. Nazi organisations had been established to oversee every aspect of the nation's life and represent the interests of youth, women, teachers, civil servants and members of the medical profession, to name but a few. Terror and intimidation tactics were exercised by the SA, SS and the Gestapo, creating a climate of fear. Relentless propaganda initiatives sought to indoctrinate everyone in Nazi ideology, while a programme of tight censorship prevented the circulation of alternative messages. "Un-German" books were burned and "degenerate" works of art and music were banned. The Nazis were tightening their grip. Yet despite all this historians have long debated the means by which the Third Reich actually functioned, and the precise role of Hitler within it. Was he, as Norman Rich proclaimed, "master of the Third Reich", or was he actually a "weak dictator", as suggested by Hans Mommsen?

The question about Hitler's grasp on power arises as a result of the fundamental structure of the Nazi regime. This was a "dual state", in which traditional state organs found themselves increasingly having to work alongside Party versions of themselves. Thus, by the mid 1930s, the field of economics would come to be populated not only by the conventional Ministries for Economics and Labour, but also the Four Year Plan Office administered by Hermann

Göring and the German Labour Front (DAF) headed by Robert Ley. Each body had an overlapping job description and they would all compete with one another for resources and control over policymaking. Some Nazis held multiple offices, enabling them to build up considerable power blocs that they were determined to protect at all costs. As a consequence, lines of authority in the Third Reich were confused and chaotic and government, in the words of Jeremy Noakes, "came to resemble a war of all against all".*

Why was such a state allowed to emerge in the first place? For some historians, it was a natural result of Hitler's fervent belief in Social Darwinism. By pitching his ministers against one another, he would ensure that they would naturally compete to come up with the best possible policy initiatives – and he could be certain he had the strongest, most able people for the job. Such thinking could be seen in a letter by district party leader Max Amann:

> Herr Hitler takes the view on principle that it is not the job of party leadership to "appoint" party leaders. Herr Hitler is today more than ever convinced that the most effective fighter is the man who wins respect for himself as leader through his own achievements.**

In this way, people seeking influence in the Third

---

* Jeremy Noakes & Geoffrey Pridham (eds), *Nazism: A Documentary Reader, 1919-1945* p. 202
** Max Amann. Reproduced in Ibid.

Reich were advised to be proactive in pushing themselves forward, rather than waiting for promotion simply to be handed to them. Furthermore, by sitting back and allowing subordinates to fight it out, Hitler could be said to be employing deliberate divide-and-rule tactics. No one person was strong enough to pose a serious threat to his own position, while everyone continued to look towards the Führer for confirmation, prestige and reward. Viewed in this light, Norman Rich's concept of a "masterful" dictator bears serious consideration.

Other Intentionalist historians would agree. Scholars such as Karl-Dietrich Bracher, Eberhard Jäckel, Andreas Hillgruber and Klaus Hildebrand see Hitler as the dominant, all-powerful leader of a totalitarian regime. Indeed, for some commentators, Nazism *was* Hitler. Certainly, the Nazis' own propaganda cultivated this impression. Constitutional theorists in the Third Reich spoke, for instance, of "Führer power" that was defined as "comprehensive and total... free and independent, exclusive and unlimited".[*]

Yet other historians have not been so easily convinced. The Structuralist school of thought, typified by the likes of Martin Broszat and Hans Mommsen, argues that the confused bureaucracy of the Third Reich was not the result of any cunning strategy by Hitler, but of neglect. For these scholars, Hitler was a lazy leader who worked irregular

---

[*] Ernst Rudolf Huber, August. 1934. Reproduced in Noakes & Pridham, *Nazism, Vol. 1: The Rise to Power*, pp. 198-9.

hours and had no interest in the affairs of day-to-day government. The post-war testimony of Hitler's former adjutant, Fritz Weidemann, lent credence to this interpretation when he commented:

> He [Hitler] disliked the study of documents. I have sometimes secured decisions from him, even ones about important matters, without his ever asking to see the relevant files. He took the view that many things sorted themselves out on their own if one did not interfere.[*]

In a similar vein, the head of the Reich Chancellery, Hans Lammers, admitted in a 1938 newspaper article that it was part of his duties to keep "peripheral matters" away from Hitler.[**]

Given these working practices, Structuralists have pondered whether Hitler actually left himself open to undue influence from those around him, thereby weakening his grip on the policy direction of the Third Reich. Furthermore, suggests Hans Mommsen, the intense competition between rival factions of the Nazi state fuelled a process of "cumulative radicalisation", pushing the regime to ever-greater extremes. This, he argues, is what led to the Holocaust, rather than any coherent plan of Hitler's. It is also claimed that it was these structural weaknesses and internal contradictions within the National Socialist state that ultimately caused it to

---
[*] Quoted in Noakes & Pridham, pp. 207-8.
[**] Hans Lammers, November 1938. Reproduced in Ibid.

collapse in spring 1945.

Both sides of the argument, though, have their limitations. The Intentionalist focus on Hitler as the primary agent of Nazi policy ignores the impact of social, economic and political factors, and downplays some of the wider complicity in the crimes of the Third Reich. An emphasis on tracing Hitler's "programme" for implementing foreign and racial policy objectives lends itself to a linear narrative developed with all the benefits of hindsight, and there is also the problem that for some areas – like the decision for the Holocaust – we simply do not have clear, documentary evidence of Hitler's personal involvement.

On the other hand, the Structuralist assertion that Hitler was a weak ruler can be equally difficult to accept. This was, after all, a man who managed to lead Germany for 12 years without any serious opposition. An emphasis on internal contradictions can downplay the role of the war in eventually bringing down Nazism and, in the final analysis, there is a need to recognise that Hitler's attitude towards "ordinary", domestic government affairs was not the same as his behaviour in the realm of foreign and racial policy; he was, for instance, much more "hands on" when it came to discussing German military tactics.

So how can we reconcile these different interpretations? In 1993, Ian Kershaw offered a middle ground by introducing the concept of "working towards the Führer". The phrase was borrowed from a 1934 document penned by Werner

Willikens, a State Secretary working within the Reich Ministry of Agriculture, which pointed out that Hitler could not possibly oversee every aspect of the Nazi state all by himself. Consequently, Willikens argued, "it is the duty of everybody to try and work towards the Führer along the lines he would wish. Anyone who makes mistakes will notice it soon enough."*

In these lines, Kershaw found the means to synthesise the conventional Intentionalist and Structuralist arguments. Here we had a Hitler who relied on those around him to take the initiative and devise ways of putting his ideological ambitions into practice, yet also a Hitler who was very much the ultimate source of authority in the Third Reich. It was Hitler who set the tone, and had the power to reward those who worked hardest to fulfil his wishes. Kershaw acknowledges that the race to secure Hitler's favour "offered endless scope for barbarous initiatives" but, as the Willikens document makes clear, Hitler would intervene if things went wildly off course. In the end, the Third Reich was constructed around a concept of "charismatic authority" embodied in Hitler. He commanded such respect and loyalty that he had "no shortage of willing helpers" ready to help him achieve his ideological goals.** This was hardly the hallmark of a "weak dictator".

* Reproduced in Ian Kershaw, "'Working Towards the Führer': Reflections on the Nature of the Hitler Dictatorship", *Central European History, Vol. 2, No. 2* (1993) pp. 103-118.
** Kershaw, "Working Towards the Führer", pp. 116-118.

LEADING NAZIS

Joseph Goebbels

Goebbels joined the NSDAP in 1924 and quickly demonstrated his talents for disseminating the Nazi message through catchy slogans, brightly coloured posters and powerful public speeches. He carefully staged party rallies to generate maximum emotional impact while orchestrated beer-hall fights similarly served to capture public attention.

Goebbels became district leader for Berlin in 1926 and founded the party newspaper, *Der Angriff* (The Attack), shortly afterwards. From 1933, he became Reich Minister for Propaganda, controlling all sources of information in the Third Reich. He organised the torchlight parades on Hitler's appointment as Chancellor in 1933, oversaw the burning of "un-German" books and was intimately involved in the staging of the 1936 Berlin Olympics. Goebbels was also responsible for the development of the "Cult of the Führer" around Hitler, crafting the image of heroic leader.

In 1943, Goebbels delivered his infamous "Total War" speech, urging the German people to continue fighting and, in the aftermath of the failed bomb plot of 1944, he was appointed Plenipotentiary for Total War, responsible for doing everything possible to keep the German war machine operational. Renowned as Hitler's most loyal follower, he continued to fight till the bitter end. When the Führer himself eventually committed suicide on 30 April 1945, Goebbels was unable to contemplate a future without him. He and his wife Magda poisoned their six children before killing themselves.

Hermann Göring

A veteran First World War fighter pilot who joined the NSDAP in 1923, Göring was injured during the ill-fated Munich Putsch the same year, a fate that left him with a life-long addiction to morphine. He became President of the Reichstag from 1932 and was one of just three Nazis within Hitler's first cabinet in January 1933, serving as Minister without Portfolio and Minister of the Interior for Prussia. The latter role gave him control over the police in the largest German state, a power he was quick to exploit with the formation of the Gestapo.

Göring's power continued to grow throughout the Third Reich. He became Commander-in-Chief of the Luftwaffe in 1935 and then head of the Four Year Plan Office from 1936. Consequently, he played a major role in preparing Germany for war, and became famous for enriching himself from looted art and property during the conflict itself. Following the early military successes, he was promoted to *Reichsmarshall*, a position that gave him authority over all over commanders of the German armed forces. However, defeat at Stalingrad in 1943, combined with the inability of the air force to wipe out the British war effort, led to a decline in Göring's political fortunes and he fell from grace.

In April 1945, he attempted to assume power, having previously been named as Hitler's successor in the event of his death or incapacity to rule. This action, though, caused him to be branded a traitor. He was expelled from the Nazi Party, stripped of his offices and placed under house arrest. At the end of the war, he was arrested by the Allies and became the chief defendant at the International Military Tribunal in Nuremberg. In October 1946, he was convicted on all four counts of crimes against peace, conspiracy, war crimes and crimes against humanity. Göring was sentenced to death but evaded his captors by biting into a cyanide capsule the night before his execution was scheduled to take place.

Rudolf Hess

A former First World War infantryman who joined the NSDAP in 1920, Hess was one of the earliest supporters of the movement. He was involved in the 1923 Munich Putsch and, like Hitler, served time in prison as a result of this attempted coup. During the late 1920s, he served as Hitler's private secretary and, from 1933, acted as Deputy Führer, becoming one of the most powerful men in Nazi Germany. In this role, he frequently represented Hitler at public events and was also responsible for signing Nazi policies into law – including the notorious Nuremberg Laws of 1935 that formally stripped Jews of their German citizenship.

Hess had a longstanding interest in aviation but became increasingly frustrated when he was forbidden to serve in the Luftwaffe during the war. Left out of military discussions and wary of the dangers of opening up a two-front war, he eventually made the unilateral decision to fly to Scotland in May 1941 and try to secure peace with Britain. He was arrested and held as a prisoner of war for the remainder of the conflict before being tried at

Nuremberg with other high-profile Nazi leaders. During the proceedings, Hess claimed to be suffering from amnesia but was nevertheless ruled fit to stand trial. He was eventually convicted on two counts – crimes against peace and conspiracy – and sentenced to life imprisonment in Spandau Prison. He committed suicide there in 1987, aged 93.

Reinhard Heydrich

One of the key figures behind the Holocaust, Heydrich began his Nazi career in 1931 when Heinrich Himmler tasked him with establishing an intelligence wing to the SS. The resulting *Sicherheitsdienst* (SD – Security Service) would be responsible for rooting out political enemies and, from 1934, Heydrich combined this role with heading up the Gestapo.

In 1938, he played a crucial role in orchestrating the *Kristallnacht* pogrom against the Jews. It was during the war, though, that his power really came to the fore. In September 1939, he was appointed head of the Reich Security Main Office (RSHA) – an organisation that united the security and criminal police. From September 1941, Heydrich also became Protector of Bohemia and Moravia (the present day Czech Republic), where he was required to "Germanise" the population. This involved mass arrests of partisans, the use of Czech slave labour and the suppression of Czech cultural activities.

Elsewhere, Heydrich and Himmler oversaw the operation of the *Einsatzgruppen* (mobile killing squads) in eastern Europe and, in the summer of 1941, Heydrich was further charged with the task of devising a "final solution to the Jewish Question". On 20 January 1942, he chaired the infamous Wannsee Conference which detailed the arrangements for the physical extermination of European Jewry. In May 1942, Heydrich's car was blown up by members of the Czechoslovak resistance and he died of his injuries a week later. In death, he was commemorated by the Nazi regime as a true martyr to the cause, receiving a grand state funeral. The construction of the first three purpose-built extermination camps at Belzec, Sobibor and Treblinka became codenamed "Operation Reinhard" in his honour, while the inhabitants of two Czech villages were slaughtered in a brutal act of reprisal for his assassination.

Heinrich Himmler

The Reichsführer of the SS who was directly responsible for the Holocaust and harboured a fervent belief in the "mastery" of the "Aryan" race, Himmler joined the NSDAP in 1923 and, like Hess and Göring, had been involved in the failed Munich Putsch. In 1925, he joined the fledgling SS that was responsible for Hitler's personal security and, over the next few years, transformed this body into a major force. The power of the SS was consolidated in 1934 with the Night of the Long Knives which crushed its rival paramilitary organisation, the SA. In the same year, responsibility for the Gestapo passed from Göring to Himmler, with the latter becoming chief of all German police. He also exercised control over the expanding concentration camp system.

During the war, Himmler was charged with enacting the "Germanisation" of eastern Europe – the expulsion of indigenous populations to make way for so-called "ethnic Germans". He established the *Einsatzgruppen* units that committed mass murder along the Eastern Front and oversaw the construction of purpose-built extermination centres to kill the Jews.

Himmler is known to have visited some of these sites in person and, on 4 October 1943, delivered a chilling speech at Posen in which he not only referred explicitly to the extermination process, but also praised his SS men for performing these duties. During the final throes of the war, Himmler was charged with the creation of the *Volkssturm* (People's Storm) – a ragtag militia that constituted a last-ditch effort to stave off approaching Soviet forces. When his military tactics proved less than effective, Himmler began independently to sue for peace. An enraged Hitler promptly labelled him a traitor and expelled him from the NSDAP. Himmler then attempted to go into hiding but was captured by the British in May 1945 and committed suicide in custody.

Portrait of Heinrich Himmler, 1938

TEN FACTS ABOUT
THE THIRD REICH

1.
The term 'The Third Reich' was first used by a German philosopher and author, Arthur Moeller van den Bruck, in his book *Das Dritte Reich*. The book was hugely influential in German ideology. In it, Moeller writes that there were two Reichs prior to Hitler's party, the first being the Holy Roman Empire and the second the German Empire from 1871-1918.

2.
Many senior Nazi leaders were keen supporters of animal rights and conservation. Animal testing was banned and schools taught the importance of animal protection. Adolf Hitler was a vegetarian.

3.
A Polish doctor, Eugene Lazowski, saved an estimated 8,000 Jews from the Nazis. Lazowski injected sick patients with OX19, a dead strain of bacteria that, when tested in blood samples, showed falsely that those injected had the often fatal Thyphus disease. Fear of disease stopped Nazis from visiting both the sick rooms in the ghettos and the surrounding villages, saving thousands of lives.

4.
The Nazis believed smoking to be detrimental to the health and banned it on public transport and in restaurants. Some health movements also believed that it was harmful to the unborn babies of pregnant women, and increased the risk of miscarriage, a proven fact today.

5.
The Swastika symbol had roots dating back 12,000 years before the Nazis placed it on their flag. Its name comes from the Sanskrit word *Svastika*, meaning 'well-being' or 'good fortune', and it remains a sacred symbol to Buddhists and Hindus. Following its use by the Nazis the swastika is now illegal in Germany.

6.
The head of the Gestapo, Heinrich Müller, disappeared the day after Hitler's suicide in his bunker in Berlin. He has never been found and his fate remains unknown.

7.
Although it is hard to calculate the exact number of Holocaust deaths, it is thought that between five and six million Jews, more than three million Soviet Prisoners of War, more than four million Soviet, Polish and Yugoslav citizens and around 70,000 sufferers from physical and mental health difficulties died as a result of Nazi atrocities.

8.
Dwight D. Eisenhower predicted that many Nazi crimes during the Holocaust would be denied. In 1945 he ordered hundreds of photos to be taken in Germany so that the evidence of Nazi crimes would be properly documented.

9.
Coco Chanel, the fashion icon who created the 'Little Black Dress', was reportedly also a Nazi spy, recruited after she had an affair with a German officer, Baron von Dinklage. She was chosen because of her close relationship with Winston Churchill.

10.
The Nazis tested a drug called Pervitin on soldiers during the 1939 German invasion of Poland. The drug was methamphetamine-based, and was a strain of the street drug known today as 'Crystal Meth'. It suppressed feelings of tiredness, and had a euphoric effect upon soldiers. After the success of the drug in 1939, the German army ordered 35 million pills for soldiers to use before their progression into France.

Life in the Third Reich

How successful was Nazi domestic policy?

Throughout the election campaigns of 1928-1933, the NSDAP had routinely presented itself as a party of the masses, offering something for everyone. Once in power, its leader had to deliver on these promises and win over the sections of society that had hitherto been sceptical about him. The extent to which he achieved this, or succeeded in transforming German society, has been the subject of sustained historical investigation.

The first challenge facing the Nazi regime was to restore the faltering German economy. With more than six million Germans registered unemployed, a "battle for work" commenced. A four-pronged approach was adopted. First, a massive public works programme was introduced, famously tasking an army of labourers with the construction of a vast motorway network (the *Autobahn*) but also ploughing millions of Reichsmarks into railways, housing projects, utilities and land improvement schemes. Second, Jews and political opponents were dismissed from posts in the civil service, immediately demonstrating the discriminatory practices of this new regime. Third, the introduction of marriage loans gave women a financial incentive to give up work and raise a family instead. Their posts would then be given to unemployed men. Finally, compulsory Reich Labour Service was introduced from June 1935 for young men aged between 18 and 25. This initiative was designed to teach young Germans the value of work, provide skills training, and promote discipline and physical fitness; it basically became another form of paramilitary training.

Collectively, these measures ensured that, by 1935, unemployment had fallen to 2.9 million and, by 1939, was just 301,900. On the surface, this reads as an example of a successful domestic policy – and Nazi propaganda was certainly quick to celebrate these rapid achievements. In reality, there is a debate as to how much of the economic recovery was driven by the Nazis, and how much

THE "CULT OF THE FÜHRER"

From the start, Nazism seemed to be embodied entirely by Adolf Hitler. Early election posters presented him as Germany's only saviour, depicted in armour to suggest heroic chivalry or bathed in heavenly light to denote Divine approval for his mission. These quasi-religious trappings continued throughout his rule, giving rise to a veritable "Cult of the Führer". Ordinary Germans could buy reproductions of his portrait to hang in their home, or collect postcards and busts of a man who was simultaneously treated as a god-like hero and a "man of the people". All of this contributed to the image of a strong, focused leader.

The "Führer Cult" was predicated on several recurring themes. First, Hitler was presented as the embodiment of order, justice and morality. He was someone who could

was the result of measures introduced by Hitler's predecessors finally making themselves felt. The figures also fail to provide the full picture: Jews, having been stripped of their citizenship, were excluded from the "official" register.

The "dignity of labour" was highly celebrated in the Third Reich. From 1933, the Nazis introduced annual May Day festivities urging people to take pride in their contribution to the national cause. Rather cynically, the regime chose the very next day, 2 May 1933, to announce a ban on trade unions, eliminating the right to strike that had been embedded in the old Weimar constitution. While the DAF – the new, state-controlled German Labour Front – was supposed to supersede the old

---

reunite the country again after years of turmoil and act decisively against those who would seemingly do Germany ill. At the same time, incidents such as the Night of the Long Knives enabled him to be shown – ironically – as a moderate figure, quick to take action against the radical elements of his own Party when they threatened to disrupt society. Indeed, it was this aspect of his rule that enabled many Germans to spare him from criticism up until defeat at Stalingrad in 1943.

Second, it was claimed that Hitler did not rule out of any personal ambition, but devoted his life to serving the nation. This again enabled him to be rendered distinct from other leading Nazis, who were becoming renowned for their petty squabbling and corruption. It also sent an important message to the rest of the population: if Hitler was willing to sacrifice all other interests for the greater good of Germany, so should they. This was important unifying glue for the *Volksgemeinschaft* and a rallying call that would become

unions, workers were left with no real outlet for expressing their grievances. There were continual grumblings about long hours, low wages and high food prices but, for the most part, fear of denunciation by their fellow workers ensured that factory life became quite atomised.

As well as providing jobs, the Nazis also aimed to improve working and living conditions for "ordinary" Germans. The "Beauty of Labour" scheme promoted better lighting, ventilation, washing facilities, rest areas and canteens in the workplace, and encouraged the creation of more green spaces around factory buildings. Meanwhile, the "Strength Through Joy" (KdF) programme served to provide better leisure opportunities for workers. This comprised a host of sporting

---

especially important during the war years.

Finally, Hitler was celebrated for his outstanding policy successes. He was held up as the instigator of Germany's "economic miracle" during the 1930s, swiftly tackling unemployment and improving standards of living – aspects for which the public could feel extremely grateful. In the field of foreign policy, he was depicted as the defender of German interests, winning added prestige as he began overturning the Treaty of Versailles and encouraging a reputation as a military genius amid the Blitzkrieg phase of the Second World War.

The propaganda myth constructed around Hitler served the regime for many years. The trouble was that, in the end, Hitler came to believe his own hype, refusing, for instance, to listen to strategy advice from the army leadership. And when the war effort took a turn for the worse from 1943, the image that had been so carefully cultivated started to unravel. ∎

activities, reflecting the regime's determination to improve the physical fitness of the nation, and a wide variety of cultural events, including concerts, cabarets, theatre performances, film screenings and special exhibitions. KdF also invited more Germans than ever before to participate in package holidays, cruises or hiking adventures, and oversaw the production of the much-hyped *Volkswagen* (People's Car) that was supposed to expand the population's sense of freedom and independence even further. All of these measures were presented as evidence of Germany's progress under Hitler, but also constituted yet another attempt at indoctrination. The state's growing incursion into people's leisure time was supposed to leave them with no space to think about alternative ideas.

The overall success of these schemes is questionable. By 1938, some 54.5 million people had participated in some form of KdF cultural activity, and those who went on a KdF sponsored holiday seem to have had a positive experience. A report from April 1939 noted: "anyone who has never made a trip in his life and sees the sea for the first time is much impressed. The effect is: 'The Nazis have done some good things after all.'"[*] Yet these packages were not quite as readily available as the propaganda made out. Some workers' wages were barely enough to cover daily essentials, let alone a trip abroad, and so, despite all the talk

---

[*] SOPADE report, April 1939. Reproduced in Noakes & Pridham, *Nazism, Vol 2: State, Economy & Society*, p. 352.

about creating a more equal society, it was the managers or the most skilled workers who reaped most benefit from the KdF.

Nazi policies towards women proved equally complicated. Rejecting the image of the so-called "New Woman" of the Weimar Republic, a character who worked, smoked, drank and enjoyed single life, Nazi ideology harked back to traditional gender roles and the primary concept of women as being dutiful wives and mothers. Older concepts of "separate spheres" were revived: the public world of politics and work was for the men; the private world of the home was for the women. Yet, as Hitler was quick to point out, these spheres were considered equally important for securing the nation's survival. Women, he argued, would be fighting for Germany just as much as male soldiers as they struggled to bring new life into the world.

A veritable cult of motherhood was duly created with annual Mother's Day celebrations and the awarding of bronze, silver and gold Motherhood Crosses to women who bore four or more children. The Nazi Women's Organisation ran courses for women to learn how to cook and manage a household while education for young girls was increasingly geared towards preparation for motherhood. The state worked to improve antenatal facilities and healthcare for nursing mothers and young infants, while at the same time banning birth control and abortions for "racially healthy" Germans. Indeed, Nazi population policy was a mixture of positive and negative eugenics. As Goebbels pointed out, "the goal is not children at any cost, but racially worthy, physically and mentally unaffected children".* Thus, marriage loans and other forms of financial support were only available to couples declared both "racially pure" and politically reliable.

In July 1933, the Law for the Prevention of Hereditarily Diseased Offspring was passed, a measure that allowed for the compulsory sterilisation of people deemed to be suffering from a congenital disease. The criteria for this was left deliberately vague, encompassing everything from schizophrenia to depression, epilepsy, deafness and chronic alcoholism. So even people who might otherwise have viewed themselves as intrinsically "German" were treated as a potential threat to the nation's health.

Population figures for the Third Reich reveal that the number of live births did, indeed, grow from 971,174 in 1933, to 1.4 million by 1939. The statistics alone cannot prove the impact of Nazi policy initiatives, however. It is questionable, for instance, how many German women saw having children as a patriotic or political act, and how much was determined by other factors such as a recovering economy making it more affordable to start a family. At the same time, there was a significant tension

---

* Cited in Gisela Bock, "Antinatalism, Maternity and Paternity in National Socialist Racism", David Crew (ed.), *Nazism and German Society, 1933-1945* (London: Routledge, 1994) p.120.

between Nazi ideology and the reality of daily life. Not every woman could afford not to work, and the demographic imbalance that hung over Germany from the First World War meant that not every woman could get married. Consequently, many remained in the work force, albeit encouraged to operate within the caring professions such as nursing or teaching. Some women found a public role for themselves, like Gertrud Scholtz-Klink who headed up the Nazi Women's Organisation. Others continued to break the mould by participating in traditionally male preserves. Hanna Reitsch, for instance, was a renowned test pilot for the German air force. It should also be remembered that some women played a very active role in the crimes of the Third Reich, facilitating the sterilisation and later murder of "racial enemies" and serving as concentration camp guards.

The real contradictions in Nazi policy, though, came during the Second World War. Faced with an acute labour shortage, the regime debated long and hard how best to staff munitions factories. Given the preferred emphasis on motherhood, there was reluctance to conscript female labour, despite the boost this might have given the war effort. In the end, it was lower-class women who bore the brunt of the work; married middle-class women were not compelled to register for labour service and this, again, raises questions about the regime's ability to enact the thorough social revolution it had promised.

Finally, German youth constituted another vital

Girls who waited for hours on Wilhelmplatz, Berlin, to greet Hitler as leader of the united German Nation after the Anschluss in 1938. Thousands lined the streets

interest group in the Third Reich. The Nazis were determined to secure the long-term future of their Reich by indoctrinating every German in National Socialist values from an early age. This was done partly through education, with school textbooks being rewritten to deliver racist messages, and partly through a more general cultural indoctrination. Illustrated books, magazines, board games and toys were all developed to appeal to different age ranges. Young boys, for instance, were encouraged to read exciting tales of derring-do in which war was an adventure and it was noble to die for one's country.

It was the Hitler Youth movement, though, that constituted the state's main effort to win over the younger generation, aspiring to deliver physical, intellectual and moral instruction according to the Nazi world view. The Hitler Youth was created as early as 1926 and steadily took over all existing youth groups in Germany, although membership did not become compulsory until 1939. The movement was split into four subsections: the Junior Hitler Youth and the Young Girls' League catered for boys and girls respectively aged between 10 and 14, while the Hitler Youth and the German Girls' League was for those aged 14-18. Each group engaged in similar activities: there was an emphasis on physical fitness, sports and outdoor activities. Members went on hikes and camping trips, learned Nazi songs and recited various ideological texts. The youth were also engaged in some of the state's big charity drives, raising money for the Winter Aid scheme and organising the collection of paper, clothing, scrap metal and rubber during the war years.

At first, Hitler Youth activities seemed to enjoy great success. Youngsters joined up, keen to escape parental control and exercise a new-found sense of independence. The novelty of some of the activities was exciting, and many testimonies from former members talk of their sense of pride at putting their uniform on for the first time. Membership conferred respect and prestige, and generated a sense of camaraderie between the children. Not everyone embraced the movement, however. Some signed up with an eye to their future career prospects, aware that a failure to join in might make them ineligible for certain jobs further down the track. Others quickly grew tired of the relentless drills, marching and bullying that came with their membership. As increasing demands were put on the Hitler Youth, especially during the war years, there was also growing frustration about just how much of their free time the movement consumed.

Similarly, much of the gloss was taken off the organisation once membership was made compulsory. Far from providing a sense of adventure, the Hitler Youth now seemed just another example of

THE VOLKSGEMEINSCHAFT

One of the central components of Nazi ideology was the belief in a *Volksgemeinschaft* – or "People's Community". This was a utopian vision of society in which class divisions had been eradicated and all "national comrades" were equal, united in their love of the Führer and through common blood ties. It was a racially-defined community with membership open to "pure" Germans only. A common identity was to be forged through a shared language, shared cultural traditions and a shared memory of the social stresses provoked by the First World War, political upheaval and economic crisis. All of this was bound up in a mythologised version of the past, the commemoration of ancient German heroes and a strong sense of a "traditional" homeland that included those territories cast asunder by the Treaty of Versailles.

The peasant farmer became one of the most iconic

control. Subcultures began to emerge as young Germans rebelled against their parents and the state. At one end of the spectrum, this involved groups like the Swing Youth who listened to banned jazz music. At the other, youth revolt took more serious action – engaging in acts of sabotage during the war years or distributing anti-Nazi pamphlets.

Overall, Nazi social policy comprised a mixture of successes and failures. On the one hand, the regime gave people hope and a new sense of security. Order was restored and crime rates were low; Germany seemed to be a safer place to live for many "ordinary" people. Propaganda elevated the

symbols of the Volksgemeinschaft: a physically fit and rugged individual rendered healthy by years of outdoor work. Divorced from the perceived degeneracy of urban living, this character was frequently depicted in visual propaganda wearing simple clothing and wielding traditional tools. He was held up as the ideal racial specimen, living off the land and raising large families; an image that reflected not only the Nazi drive to raise the birth rate, but also offered a potent metaphor about Germany's own fertility and rebirth.

The Volksgemeinschaft was conceived as a two-way process. The Nazi state would provide for its members, striving to improve living and working conditions and establishing new welfare schemes to aid those in need. In return, the people were expected to prove themselves worthy of community membership, conforming to the National Socialist state, putting the nation's interests ahead of their own and working together to rebuild Germany.

Nazi propaganda repeatedly extolled the virtues of hard work, dedication, courage and self-sacrifice, while the Gestapo took a special interest in anyone who shirked their duties. The extent to which the Nazis actually achieved their

social status of workers and mothers, giving people a sense of pride even if they were not always materially better off. On the other hand, whatever benefits people may have reaped from the state came at the expense of personal freedoms and the vicious persecution of anyone who did not fulfil the necessary racial criteria.

How widespread was German resistance to Hitler?

In the aftermath of the Second World War most Germans understandably tried to distance vision, though, has been disputed. Certainly, evidence from the period suggests that there remained a number of class-based grievances, especially during the Second World War when middle-class women were criticised for not doing their fair share of the war work.

Clearer evidence of the impact of the Volksgemeinschaft can be seen in the treatment of so-called "community aliens". Not everyone was allowed to be a member of the community; Jews, Sinti, Roma and other ethnic minorities were automatically excluded on grounds of race and subject to ever-greater persecution as a result. Those who transgressed social norms or were seen as not pulling their weight were also denied access to welfare support and increasingly pushed out of public life.

This included the "workshy", vagrants, alcoholics, prostitutes, petty criminals and homosexuals. Collectively, these social outsiders were deemed "unfit" and subject to violence, internment in concentration camps, forced abortions, compulsory sterilisation and, ultimately, even murder. Domestic policy in the Third Reich, therefore, cannot be separated from the broader issue of race. ∎

themselves from the Third Reich, pointing to the fact they had Jewish friends or highlighting passive acts of opposition against the regime. At official level, the ruling parties of the two German states also drew carefully upon a legacy of resistance to underpin their own legitimacy. East Germany, a Communist state allied to Moscow, accordingly stressed the role of the radical Left in challenging Hitler with memorials and history books celebrating the heroism of KPD members who had suffered in the concentration camps.

West Germany, headed by the conservative Konrad Adenuaer, put its stock in commemorating German military resistance. The accuracy of these post-war representations, however, has been disputed. In the 1960s, Hans Mommsen used the phrase "resistance without the people" to suggest a lack of popular opposition to Nazism. This interpretation was subsequently challenged by other historians who delved into case studies of particular regions or social groups and pointed to a much wider range of dissenting activities. This begged the question: how should we actually define resistance when looking at the Third Reich?

Clearly, the term "resistance" should not be taken lightly. The Nazis, of course, would label *all* acts of defiance as "resistance", even if it was something as trivial as failing to give the Hitler salute, or telling an anti-Hitler joke. However, as Ian Kershaw points out, it is important to distinguish between opposition to an individual policy, and opposition to the Nazi state as a whole. On closer inspection, it seems that most people were able to criticise some aspects of the Third Reich without losing their fundamental faith in Hitler or the basic concept of National Socialism. Some historians, such as Walter Hofer, thus suggest that the only meaningful use of the term "resistance" is when it is applied to acts aimed specifically at destroying the Nazi regime. Such an approach concentrates on *active* rather than passive protest.

During the Third Reich, there were four main sources for potential opposition or resistance. The first came from the Left and the industrial workers that made up its traditional constituency. Both the social democratic SPD and the communist KPD were driven underground following Hitler's appointment as chancellor, but this did not prevent them distributing anti-Nazi pamphlets and newspapers. The Gestapo, though, were always on their tail and, after waves of arrests by 1938, the SPD eventually decided that such activity was too dangerous. Their focus switched to information-gathering, with a network of members producing regular reports on public opinion and the state of the country. The KPD, meanwhile, spawned several smaller groups including the Red Orchestra which passed German military secrets to the Soviet Union before being discovered by the Gestapo.

The most high-profile act of resistance undertaken by an individual worker, meanwhile, was Georg Elser's attempt to assassinate Hitler in

November 1939. Aggrieved by the regime's erosion of workers' rights, Elser planted a bomb in a Munich beer cellar where Hitler was due to give a speech. The Führer, however, was delayed in reaching the venue and missed the blast. Elser was captured by the Gestapo and executed for high treason.

Elsewhere, some factory workers engaged in absenteeism, "go slow" practices or acts of sabotage against their equipment, with unrest increasing during the last months of the war. These remained relatively isolated acts, however; there was no unified uprising among the working class.

The second key group comprised the churches, institutions with a sizable following and, arguably, a moral obligation to speak out against the regime. Certainly there were notable moments of church-related opposition. A breakaway group of Protestants known as the Confessing Church challenged Nazi interference in clerical affairs, with several prominent clergymen placed under house arrest or interned in concentration camps as a result. Their fate sparked an outpouring of public support as their congregations held vigils, signed petitions, refused to contribute to the Winter Aid Scheme and threatened to resign their membership of the NSDAP. Meanwhile, German Catholic protest was evident in 1936 when the regime attempted to remove crucifixes from schools, and in 1941 when Bishop Clemens August Graf von Galen led the revolt against the so-called "euthanasia" scheme that was killing disabled people.

In each of these cases, the wave of public sympathy with the clergy forced the regime to back down, demonstrating what could be achieved if enough people raised their voices. Indeed, a Nazi police report admitted their inability to dissolve old confessional loyalties: "the influence of the Church on the population is so strong that the National Socialist spirit cannot penetrate".[*]

The German churches failed to capitalise on their potential, however. There was no institutional condemnation of the Nazi regime or the persecution of ethnic minorities; it was left to individual church leaders to make a stand. Furthermore, both denominations shared in some of the National Socialist ideology, including anti-semitism, and the opposition that did occur was frequently a response to Nazi attacks on church power. Some scholars have gone even further, suggesting that the solace that the church was able to provide to Nazi perpetrators makes them complicit in facilitating the crimes of the Third Reich.

The third, oft-cited source for resistance came from German youth. Despite the regime's best efforts, it failed to indoctrinate completely the younger generation and a number of cliques developed in opposition to the Hitler Youth movement. While police reports reveal that the regime viewed all of these subgroups as provocative,

---

[*] Police report cited in Ian Kershaw, *Popular Opinion & Political Dissent in the Third Reich: Bavaria, 1933-1945* (Oxford, 1983) pp.200-1.

it is questionable to what extent the Swing Youth – a group of disaffected teenagers listening to banned jazz records – constituted a genuine act of political "resistance", rather than simple adolescent rebellion against mainstream culture. More significant in terms of active opposition were the Edelweiss Pirates, a group of youngsters based near Cologne who engaged in acts of sabotage during the war and distributed Allied propaganda; and the White Rose movement of university students which was based in Munich. The latter was led by Hans and Sophie Scholl and produced numerous pamphlets that vehemently condemned Nazi crimes, including the persecution of the Jews, and urged the German population to rise up against the Nazi state. For each group, the reprisals were severe. A crackdown on the Pirates in autumn 1944 resulted in 16 members being publicly hanged. Members of the White Rose group were arrested in 1943, tried before the notorious People's Court, and executed by guillotine.

Finally, the most notorious example of resistance against the Nazi regime came from conservative army officers and members of military intelligence with the July Bomb Plot of 1944. Codenamed "Operation Valkyrie" and led by Claus von Stauffenberg, the aim was to assassinate Hitler in the Wolf's Lair (a military headquarters in occupied Poland), take over the government and negotiate a surrender with the Allies. The plan went awry. The bomb had been concealed in a briefcase which was moved at the last minute, leaving Hitler with minor injuries. Attempts to launch a coup back in Berlin likewise collapsed and the conspirators were duly arrested and executed.

While the bomb plot has been much celebrated in popular culture, it is important to remember that it only occurred when the war was already going badly for Germany; the same men had been happy to reap the rewards of Nazism during the earlier period of rapid victories and many of them actually shared some of the tenets of Nazi ideology. Stauffenberg, for instance, betrayed his own racism when he wrote to his wife while stationed in Poland. "The population here," he commented, "is an unbelievable rabble. There are a lot of Jews and a lot of crossbreeds."[*] Likewise, the conspirators were not seeking to replace Hitler with democracy but another authoritarian regime. Thus it was not so much *Nazism* that they were resisting as a poorly-executed military campaign.

Active resistance aiming to destroy the Nazi state was thus in relatively short supply, accounting for less than one per cent of the German population. In the end, it was the external might of the advancing Allies that brought the regime down, rather than any popular uprising. What opposition there was stemmed from individuals rather than institutions, and was often directed by self-interest rather than wider humanitarian concerns.

[*] Cited in Martyn Housden, *Resistance and Conformity in the Third Reich* (London: Routledge, 1997) p. 100.

Resistance, though, was inherently limited by the very organisation of the Nazi state. Hitler's grip on power ensured that there was no obvious rival to challenge him from inside the National Socialist movement. There was no functioning parliament to question him, nor any legal political parties to mount an effective opposition against legislation. Above all, the Third Reich was a terror state and concerns for self-preservation understandably loomed large for most people. The threat of the concentration camps served as one form of deterrent while the fear of denunciation by friends, colleagues, neighbours or even relatives worked against the formation of any large-scale opposition movement.

THE TERROR STATE

The Third Reich was renowned for its use of terror, symbolised primarily by the SS and the Gestapo. The SS had initially been formed as Hitler's personal bodyguard but continually expanded during the Third Reich until it controlled the whole police and security system.

Headed by Heinrich Himmler, it was the SS's task to create the Nazis' vision of a "racially pure" Germany. Consequently, the SS were intimately involved in rounding up so-called "enemies of the Reich", organising the deportations of the Jews and administering the entire concentration camp network. The Gestapo, or secret police, were part of this SS machinery, responsible for rooting out political opponents and any other signs of dissent.

Both institutions acted outside the law and had a free rein to take people into "protective custody", torture them and imprison without trial.

The KPD, for instance, had to keep its underground cells as small as possible to try and avoid detection by the Gestapo – and this ensured that opposition forces remained weak and fractured. At the same time, we cannot overlook the fact that Hitler was genuinely popular with the German people. While there may have been grumbling about food prices or working conditions at times, or state regulations, many people were able to overlook these issues and concentrate on the fact that, under the Nazis, there was economic recovery, political stability, low crime rates and great foreign policy successes. Under these circumstances, it is no wonder that few saw any reason to upset the applecart.

Their victims included trade unionists, communists, homosexuals, Jehovah's Witnesses and anyone who was alleged to have expressed anti-Nazi sentiments. In short, all sectors of the population could become the subject of a police enquiry.

Despite its name, the Gestapo was anything but secret. It was only too happy to publicise details of arrests and punishments to serve as a deterrent to others and perpetuate its self-image as an omnipotent force whose tentacles reached into all aspects of German society. It created a climate of fear; people had to exercise great caution as to what they said and who they met, never knowing who might be observing them.

The impact of the SS and the Gestapo cannot be denied. Some 225,000 Germans were convicted of political crimes between 1933 and 1939 alone – and the use of terror was heightened even further during the Second World War. However, the means by which the Gestapo operated have been debated over the years by historians. Most notably, Robert Gellately argues that, despite its reputation, the

Foreign policy

Did Hitler plan to go to war?

It was evident from the start that the Nazis had some big foreign policy ambitions. The reversal of the Treaty of Versailles and the pursuit of *Lebensraum* occupied the first three points of the NSDAP's 25 point programme and had been discussed at length in *Mein Kampf.* Consequently, once Hitler had consolidated his power over Germany by mid 1934, he duly set about expanding his remit beyond the nation's existing borders. In 1935, he reintroduced conscription and launched a

---

Gestapo was actually woefully underfunded and under-staffed. To function, it was heavily reliant on denunciations volunteered by members of the public – meaning that the German people were effectively policing themselves. Gestapo files from the city of Wurzburg, for instance, reveal that 54 per cent of investigations launched into cases of "race defilement" – "Aryans" having relationships with Jews, Poles or other minorities – originated from reports received from the population.

Some denunciations stemmed from ideological convictions but the majority seem to have been the result of self-interest – a means to remove a business competitor or settle a neighbourhood dispute. Spite and jealousy were key motivating factors for informants. Overall, it seems that many people managed to adjust themselves to state terror and found ways to work with it. Consequently, the Third Reich could be said to have ruled through a mixture of consent and coercion. ■

Opposite: Hitler broadcasting a speech over the radio, 5 September 1934

not-so-secret rearmament programme. In 1936, he charged Hermann Göring with overseeing the Four Year Plan, a drive to ensure that the nation would be ready for war by 1940. Having witnessed the devastating effects of the Allied blockade during the First World War, the Nazi leaders were determined that this time the country would be as self-sufficient as possible.

In 1936, Hitler also embarked upon his first expansionist manoeuvre, ordering troops into the supposedly demilitarised Rhineland. This was a direct challenge to the post-war peace settlement and the first test of the Allies' willingness to uphold it. When they turned a blind eye, reasoning that Germany had a right to go into "her own backyard", Hitler was left triumphant, and confidently began to push his luck even further.

Over the next three years, the Third Reich continued to expand: 1938 brought the longed-for *Anschluss* (union) with Austria, followed by the German-speaking Sudetenland of Czechoslovakia, the latter territory handed over to Germany by Britain and France at the Munich Conference in an effort to avoid war. While the British Prime Minister Neville Chamberlain was confident that this deal had secured "peace for our time", Hitler was not yet sated. In March 1939, German troops invaded the rest of Czechoslovakia. By September, they had turned their attention to Poland. This time, though, Britain and France would not renege on their promise to protect a smaller country and the Second World War erupted on 3 September 1939. The conflict in Europe would last until May 1945, with devastating results.

Did Hitler actually want war? Certainly, the post-war trials saw the remnants of the Nazi leadership indicted for crimes against peace and conspiracy, and the prosecution spent a lot of time trying to prove that there had been a "blueprint for aggression". Intentionalist historians have likewise emphasised the central role of Hitler in foreign policy decisions, and the consistency of his aims. Both *Mein Kampf* and Hitler's lesser-known

---

THE NAZI–SOVIET PACT

One famously contradictory element of Nazi foreign policy concerns the ten-year non-aggression pact that was signed with the Soviet Union on 23 August 1939. The two nations were completely ideologically opposed to one another, and their mutual antipathy was well-known. This sudden union was consequently greeted with international astonishment.

On the one hand, the Nazi-Soviet pact can be held up as evidence that Nazi foreign policy was confused and that Hitler simply took advantage of situations on an ad hoc basis. On the other hand, there was a real pragmatism at work here. The deal enabled Germany to receive vital raw materials from the USSR and, most significantly, avoid fighting any future war on two fronts. The USSR benefitted too, gaining extra time for rearmament and – under a secret protocol – new territory in the Baltic states.

It was a series of short-term factors that brought the pact into being. The Danzig crisis of March 1939 had increased

Zweites Buch (*Second Book*) repeatedly outlined his desire for *Lebensraum* and the establishment of a "Greater Germany" based on racial ties. Furthermore, they argue, it was clear that Hitler envisaged this extra "living space" in the East, necessitating a war of conquest against the Soviet Union.

Some historians, such as Andreas Hillgruber, go even further, suggesting that expansion in Europe was just the beginning and that Hitler's ultimate aim was to achieve global domination. Whatever the end goal, though, the Intentionalists agree that Hitler had a "master plan" and stuck firmly to his

---

Soviet fears of an immediate German threat to eastern Europe, while the west's policy of appeasement prompted concerns that the USSR, like Czechoslovakia, might be left to bear the brunt of Nazism alone. Attempts to organise an Anglo-French-Soviet front against Germany repeatedly broke down, hampered by suspicions of one another's motives.

The fact that such meetings were taking place at all, though, aroused concerns among the Germans that they might end up surrounded. Rather than sit back and wait for that to happen, the Nazis adopted a proactive approach that demonstrated Hitler's ability as a strategist.

First, he took care to dispatch his Foreign Minister, Joachim von Ribbentrop, to Moscow to negotiate personally with his Russian counterpart. This contrasted with earlier Anglo-Soviet meetings to which the British had sent lower-ranking Foreign Office staff who were not empowered to make crucial decisions.

Second, Ribbentrop travelled directly by plane, demonstrating the urgency and importance that the Nazis were attaching to the discussions. During the last round of Anglo-French meetings with the USSR, the western diplomats had travelled by sea, taking four

stated aims. The establishment of the Four Year Plan in 1936 seems to back this up, with Hitler ordering that the Germany army be operational and the German economy fit for war "within four years". His envisaged timing was off by just a few months due to the Allies taking their stand over Poland.

Structuralists, however, insist that Hitler had no clear programme but simply responded to opportunities as they arose. A case in point concerns his vacillating position with regard to Britain, and the argument that the German economy was not fully mobilised for war until 1942. Indeed, primary

---

days to reach their destination. Finally, Hitler sent a personal request to Stalin directly, further signalling the Third Reich's willingness to do business. This approach, combined with the strategic advantages that such a deal offered the USSR, ensured that the pact was duly signed in the early hours of 24 August 1939, less than a day after Ribbentrop's arrival in the Russian capital.

The agreement would have major implications for European history. Just one week after Russia promised to remain neutral in the face of a German attack on Poland, the Nazis attacked and the Second World War began. Hitler was then able to concentrate all his initial energies on conquering western Europe without fear of a two-front war diverting his forces. Rapid victories brought more resources into the German war effort and boosted Hitler's prestige until, in June 1941, he felt sufficiently strong to renege on his promise and launch Operation Barbarossa against the Soviet Union.

As the opposing forces of Nazism and Communism faced one another, Hitler declared that it would be a fight to the death. The Second World War had now entered a more brutal, racist and ideologically-driven phase. ∎

sources from the time of the Rhineland invasion suggest that, if confronted by Allied resistance, German troops were ordered to retreat. Likewise, historians have disputed the significance of the Hossbach Memorandum, a summary of a meeting between Hitler and his generals that took place in November 1937. Intentionalists – and the Nuremberg prosecutors – again took this document as evidence of Hitler actively planning for war. Structuralists argue that the document reflects the ad hoc nature of Nazi policy as Hitler weighed up the various contingencies he might face over the next few years. For them, the meeting was more about finding a way out of growing problems in the domestic economy than a carefully-designed strategy for war.

Other scholars have even challenged the significance of Hitler himself within German foreign policy. During the 1960s, A.J.P. Taylor posited that, rather than developing original aims and taking the country in a new direction, Hitler was merely following the foreign policy of his predecessors. In other words, Nazi actions during the 1930s were a continuation of the German aggression that had been witnessed before the First World War. Taylor's thesis was immediately challenged by other, mainly German, historians such as Gerhard Ritter who insisted that Nazism was an aberration in an otherwise healthy history, distinct from anything that had gone before.

In the end, it is probably most accurate to state

that there were certain foreign policy goals that were particularly close to Hitler's heart. The recapturing of eastern territory lost under the Treaty of Versailles was one such aim, as was further expansion to create the living space for Germany's growing population. These were goals that the regime was determined to realise as soon as it could.

It is also evident that foreign policy was inseparable from racial policy. Part of the reason that the Nazis envisaged a programme of eastwards expansion is that they viewed the indigenous population of Slavs and Poles as "inferior" and thus ripe for subjugation. That such foreign policy ambitions were likely to result in war was also recognised by the Nazi regime. From the start, propaganda was couched in military rhetoric with Germany depicted as a nation battling for survival against various imagined enemies.

Paramilitary-style training for members of the Reich Labour Service and the Hitler Youth offered further opportunities for a future conflict. While the precise timing of the Second World War may not have been entirely of Hitler's choosing it was not as if the country was taken completely by surprise and, ever the opportunist, Hitler was quick to rise to the occasion. A series of *Blitzkrieg* victories were won over Poland, France, Belgium and the Netherlands and, by 1942, the Nazis had most of continental Europe under their control.

Racial policy

How did "ordinary" Germans respond to the persecution of the Jews?

When Allied troops liberated the Nazi concentration camps in 1945, the watching world was shocked and disgusted at the immense human suffering uncovered therein. Questions immediately began to be asked as to how such atrocities were possible, and whether the German people as a whole, rather than just the immediate Nazi leadership, bore a collective guilt and responsibility for what had

VICTIMS OF NAZISM

Millions of people perished as a result of Nazi persecution. Some were considered "undesirable" because of their ethnicity or health conditions and targeted on racial grounds. Others were victimised due to their actions and beliefs.

Jews: constituted just one per cent of the German population in 1933 but became the primary focus of Nazi racial policy which escalated from a boycott of Jewish businesses, to segregation, internment, deportation and murder. Six million European Jews were killed in the Holocaust.

Sinti and Roma (Gypsies): viewed as both "asocial" due to their itinerant lifestyle and racially "inferior". This group were also deprived of their civil rights under the Nuremberg Laws and subject to internment in concentration camps. A "Central Office to Combat the Gypsy Menace" was opened in 1936 under the remit of Heinrich Himmler with the aim of coordinating anti-gypsy policy. A particularly large wave of arrests occurred just before the opening of the 1936 Berlin Olympics when

occurred. Many Germans protested that they had no idea about what was happening to the Jews and, in any case, stressed their powerlessness to intervene against the Nazi regime.

Subsequently, historians have often revisited the issue of "ordinary" people's responses to Nazi racial policy. In 1996, Daniel Goldhagen aroused fresh controversy when he suggested that the perpetrators of the Holocaust had willingly engaged in acts of mass murder. This, he claimed, was due to an innate, "eliminationist" anti-semitism within the German psyche. In other words, he suggested that Germans were somehow predisposed to hate,

---

Sinti and Roma were rounded up and placed in Marzahn, a specially-constructed concentration camp on the edge of the capital. During the Second World War, thousands of Sinti and Roma were shot by the *Einsatzgruppen* or deported to extermination camps. An estimated 90,000-150,000 killed in total.

Poles and Slavs: as the Third Reich expanded, Poles and Slavic peoples living in eastern Europe also became targets for persecution, being perceived as *Untermensch* (subhuman). Thousands were executed by the *Einsatzgruppen* as German forces made their way along the eastern front in 1941. Millions more were interned in camps or deported to Germany to become slave labourers in the factories.

Homosexuals: seen as incompatible with the Nazi concept of "normal" family life. They were stripped of their civil rights and subject to Gestapo terror, with some 15,000 men being interned in concentration camps. The Nazis believed that homosexuality was a vice that could be cured through hard work, beatings and public humiliation. Consequently, conditions for this group within the camps were particularly brutal. Many were also subject to medical experiments.

and destroy, Jews and welcomed Nazi racial policies with enthusiasm.[25] A more measured approach, however, is adopted by Ian Kershaw who sums up the response of the German population as primarily one of indifference. For Kershaw, it was the steady erosion of moral boundaries, and the failure to speak out during the first stages of discrimination, that ultimately paved the way to the creation of Auschwitz.

One of the first hints of the tough measures that would be applied to "enemies of the Reich" came

* Daniel J. Goldhagen, *Hitler's Willing Executioners: Ordinary Germans and the Holocaust* (London: Abacus, 1996).

Statistics as to the number of homosexuals killed in the camps are unavailable.

People with disabilities: targeted through the "Law for the Prevention of Hereditarily Diseased Offspring" that ordered the compulsory sterilisation of anyone considered to be "unfit". This policy covered a raft of conditions including physical deformities, mental illness and learning disabilities and affected an estimated 200,000-350,000 people. Throughout the 1930s, there was also growing propaganda that stressed the perceived "burden" that disabled people posed to the rest of society, presenting them as "useless eaters" and a drain on public resources. From autumn 1939, the regime began a policy of "euthanising" disabled children, and then extended this programme to encompass disabled adults as well. These people were killed by starvation, lethal injection or gas. The "euthanasia" programme demonstrates the complicity of the medical profession in the crimes of the Third Reich and reveals direct links with the Holocaust in terms of personnel and techniques. A total of 275,000 disabled people are believed to have been killed by 1945.

on 22 March 1933 with the opening of the first concentration camp in Dachau. Initially, this was constructed to hold political opponents and habitual criminals but it would expand over the course of the Third Reich to include ethnic minorities and other "asocials" as well. By the outbreak of war in September 1939, further camps had been established at Buchenwald, Sachsenhausen, Neuengamme, Flossenbürg, Ravensbrück and Mauthausen. The latter was based near Linz in newly annexed Austrian territory but the remainder were all situated inside Germany itself. While conditions inside these camps may have been

Jehovah's Witnesses: refused to accept the authority of the state, give the Hitler Salute or join Nazi organisations. They objected to the introduction of military service in 1935 and refused to undertake work that would support the war effort. Consequently, many were arrested and sent to concentration camps. They could be freed if they signed a document renouncing their faith but few were willing to accede to this, even under torture. An estimated 10,000 German Jehovah's Witnesses were interned at some stage or other; 1,000 of these died in the camps.

Black Germans: a wave of racist propaganda emerged after the First World War when French colonial troops were used to occupy the Rhineland. Children born of these soldiers and local German women became known as "Rhineland Bastards" and shunned by society. Even before the Nazis came to power, they were barred from certain jobs and denied the right to go to university. During the Third Reich, though, many were forcibly sterilised or subjected to medical experiments.

Asocials: other groups who were subjected to Nazi terror and internment included criminals, alcoholics, prostitutes and beggars. ∎

obscured, their existence was well known. Dachau, for instance, had opened in a blaze of publicity as the regime both celebrated its tough stance on crime and issued a warning to any other would-be transgressors. Indeed, knowledge of these camps was so ingrained that there are even accounts of young children playing at sending Communists to concentration camps.

It is, of course, important to distinguish between these sites and the purpose-built extermination camps that would appear in occupied Poland; the regime had not embarked upon the systematic murder of the Jews just yet. However, it was known that certain groups were being placed into "preventative" custody and rumours did abound about the terrible treatment being administered to them. None of this, though, served to evoke popular protest.

The first official act against the Jews came on 1 April 1933 with a one-day boycott of Jewish shops. Yet this initiative did not play out exactly as the regime had hoped. Many people refused to bow to the new directives, partly because they saw no reason to change their shopping habits on the whim of the new government, and partly because prices in some of the Jewish shops were more favourable. Some shoppers were even photographed brandishing their purchases quite brazenly in front of the SA standing guard, refusing to be intimidated.

As the Nazis consolidated their power, racial policy became more organised. From September 1935, the Nuremberg Laws came into effect, officially segregating the Jewish and non-Jewish population. Jews were stripped of their citizenship and political rights and forbidden to marry or employ non-Jews or to display the national flag. Looking at reports compiled by both the Nazis and the Social Democratic Party in Exile (SOPADE), it is evident that many "ordinary" Germans simply ignored the legislation. Some paid lip service to the directives but did not let them affect their daily interactions with local Jews. One Jewish customer, who suddenly found himself publicly excluded from his regular café,

> asked the manageress why she had not told him that he was not welcome. The manageress kept apologising and told the customer that he should stay and that she had been made to put up the notice".[*]

Reflecting on the situation in 1937, a Gestapo source admitted that a "large percentage of peasants still have business dealings with Jews... and show a complete lack of awareness of race".[**]

Between 1933 and 1937, Nazi racial policy concentrated on the legalised discrimination of those it deemed to be "other". On 9 November 1938, though, the regime entered a more radical phase with the first nation-wide wave of violence

---

[*] SOPADE report, June 1935. Reproduced in Noakes & Pridham, *Nazism, Vol. 2: State, Economy & Society*.
[**] Gestapo report, 1 August 1937. Reproduced in Noakes & Pridham, *Nazism, Vol. 2: State, Economy & Society*, pp. 546-7.

against the Jews. The *Kristallnacht* (Night of the Broken Glass) pogrom saw 250 synagogues set on fire, thousands of Jewish homes and businesses smashed and looted, and many Jews beaten and killed. The trigger for this event was the assassination of the Nazi diplomat Ernst vom Rath in Paris, killed by a young Jewish man, Herschel Grynszpan. The official line was that the pogrom was the natural, indignant reaction of the German masses, but in reality the event was orchestrated by Joseph Goebbels and Reinhard Heydrich and carried out by SA men out of uniform.

Kristallnacht offers a useful case study into German responses to Nazi racial policy. Daniel Goldhagen argues that, in small towns all over Germany, "ordinary Germans spontaneously, without provocation or encouragement, participated in the brutalities".[*] While he admits that some people were taken aback by the sudden flurry of violence in their midst, he insists that none of this diminished the population's overall enthusiasm for anti-Jewish policies. Primary sources from 1938, however, suggest a more complicated state of affairs. A report from the American Consul in Leipzig described locals being "benumbed", "aghast" and "nauseated" at the scenes but powerless to intervene against the fury of the perpetrators.[**]

Ian Kershaw's case study of Bavaria offers

---

[*] Goldhagen, *Hitler's Willing Executioners*, pp. 100-101.
[**] David Buffum, November 1938. Reproduced in Noakes & Pridham, *Nazism, Vol. 2: State, Economy & Society*, pp. 555-556.

similar conclusions. He notes that there were numerous mutterings of sympathy for the Jews, disgust at the harm being brought upon Germany's reputation, and indignity at the wanton destruction of property at a time when the population was being pressured to scrimp and save as much as possible in readiness for the coming war effort. Many of the reactions, it is true, stemmed from economic self-interest, but Kershaw has been careful to highlight individual acts of support offered to Jews in the immediate aftermath of the pogrom, with donations of food, clothing and money to victims. In the long run, however, the outrage expressed at Kristallnacht soon subsided and within weeks the majority of the population had fallen back into apathy and indifference.[*]

In the end, perhaps one of the best insights into German responses to Nazi racial policy comes from the memoir of Melita Maschmann, a former leader of the League of German Girls (the BDM). In terms of Kristallnacht, she describes how

> for the space of a second I was clearly aware that something terrible had happened there. Something frighteningly brutal. But almost at once I switched over to accepting what had happened was over and done with and avoiding

---

[*] Ian Kershaw, *Popular Opinion and Political Dissent in the Third Reich: Bavaria, 1933-45* (Oxford: Clarendon Press, 1983) pp. 257-274.

critical reflection".[*]

Like many people, she simply turned a blind eye to what was in front of her. Elsewhere in her memoir she confesses that whenever she spouted anti-Semitic slogans or heard about Jews being driven out of work and their homes, she never linked this to the plight of her Jewish schoolfriends or neighbours: "it was only *the* Jew who was being persecuted and 'made harmless'".[**] In this simple phrase, we see how people were able to go along with Nazi rhetoric without really thinking about its implications. The enemy depicted in the propaganda was a grotesque caricature that was deliberately dehumanised. This "abstract Jew" could be blamed for everything without people making the connection to actual real people they may have known personally. It is this compartmentalising that enabled the regime to keep testing the boundaries and erode moral sensibilities until it eventually reached a point where genocide could be contemplated by the Nazi leadership.

When was the decision for the "Final Solution" taken?

The Nazi persecution of the Jews passed through several phases over the course of the Third Reich.

---

[*] Melita Maschmann, *Account Rendered: A Dossier on my Former Self* (New York: Abelard-Schuman, 1965) p. 56.
[**] Ibid., pp. 40-41.

The first years of Hitler's rule, 1933-35, saw isolated acts of physical violence perpetrated by SA forces, but the primary emphasis at this time was on defining who would be classified as Jews and steadily depriving those who were of their civil liberties. As the 1930s progressed, German Jews became increasingly segregated from the rest of society while a process of "Aryanisation" stripped them of their economic interests as Jewish businesses were handed over to non-Jews.

As the Third Reich expanded to incorporate Austria and then Czechoslovakia, more and more European Jews became subject to Nazi persecution. Conditions worsened with the outbreak of the Second World War. Polish Jews were rounded up and placed in ghettos, and deportations from the rest of occupied Europe would soon follow. The invasion of the Soviet Union in June 1941 saw the German army being followed by the *Einsatzgruppen*, mobile killing squads who massacred hundreds of thousands of civilians – a series of atrocities often referred to as the "Holocaust by bullets". By the end of the year, Jews were being murdered by gas in specially converted vans and construction was in hand on a new set of purpose-built extermination camps. The mass murder of the Jews was now firmly under way.

Had Hitler always intended this? A letter from 1919 had seen him calling for the "uncompromising removal of the Jews altogether".[*] Since then, the Jew had been systematically represented as Germany's enemy, dehumanised and invariably linked to the threat of Bolshevism. Repeated references to the Jews constituting a "cancer", "racial tuberculosis" or a "parasitic" influence on the nation all added up to the same message: Germany had been infected or infested and the nation's health was under threat as a result. Pursuing this biological metaphor suggests that the "logical" conclusion in Nazi eyes would necessarily involve physical extermination. In January 1939, Hitler also warned that any outbreak of war would result in the "annihilation of the Jewish race in Europe".[**] Consequently, Intentionalist historians have concluded that the mass murder of European Jewry had been anticipated right from the start, that racial policy built up relentlessly towards this goal and that Hitler himself was the driving force behind it all.

Structuralist historians such as Hans Mommsen, Raul Hilberg and Martin Broszat, however, reject the notion that the Holocaust was predetermined. Instead, they highlight the different initiatives that were trialled during the Third Reich as evidence

---

[*] Adolf Hitler, 16 September 1919. Reproduced at Jewish Virtual Library, http://www.jewishvirtuallibrary.org/jsource/Holocaust/Adolf_Hitler's_First_Antisemitic_Writing.html

[**] Adolf Hitler, 30 January 1939. Reproduced in J. Noakes & G. Pridham (eds), *Nazism: A Documentary Reader 1919-1945. Vol. 3: Foreign Policy, War and Racial Extermination* (Exeter: University of Exeter Press, 1988) p. 1049.

that the Nazis had no idea what to do with the Jews. Throughout the 1930s, for instance, the emphasis seemed to be on emigration rather than extermination and, as late as 1940, there was a proposal to deport Jews forcibly to the French colony of Madagascar, though the war situation eventually quashed this idea.

Structuralists also concentrate less on Hitler and more on the radicalisation of Nazi policy caused by intense rivalries between leading figures of the regime, and on local initiatives being carried out by those on the ground in the occupied territories. In July 1941, for example, SS-Sturmbannführer Rolf-Heinz Höppner wrote to inform Adolf Eichmann, Head of the Office for Jewish Affairs in the Reich Security Main Office, about the appalling conditions within Polish ghettos. He volunteered the suggestion that

> serious consideration must be given as to whether the most humane solution might not be to finish off Jews who are incapable of work with some quick-acting preparation.*

If the Holocaust had not been intended from the start, when was the decision made to kill European Jewry? Reaching a definitive answer on this question is nigh on impossible. There is no surviving written order from Hitler, and it is doubtful whether

---

* Rolf-Heinz Höppner, 16 July 1941. Reproduced in Ibid., p. 1103.

one ever existed at all. What documents we do have are littered with Nazi euphemisms – with phrases such as "evacuation" and "resettlement" bandied about to disguise what was really going on. In addition, it seems that even some Nazis were confused as to the agreed course. A note from the Ministry for the Eastern Territories on 18 December 1941, for instance, was forced to concede that "the Jewish question has *probably* been clarified by now through verbal discussion".*

Structuralists, therefore, have put forward several possible suggestions over the years. Some link the decision firmly to the invasion of the Soviet Union. The so-called "Commissar Order" issued on 6 June 1941 would seem to support this, with German troops being told that partisans were to be "as a matter of principle... finished immediately with a weapon".** There was certainly a sense that this was going to be an ideologically-infused battle for survival. Others, like historian Christopher Browning, put their emphasis on the late summer-early autumn of 1941, a time when the *Einsatzgruppen* were targeting the elderly, women and children and more troops were entering the killing fields. It was also on 31 July 1941 that Reinhard Heydrich was charged with devising a

---

* Ministry for the Eastern Territories, 18 December 1941. Reproduced in Ibid., p. 1098.
** Directives for the Treatment of Political Commissars, 6 June 1941. Reproduced at German History in Documents and Images, http://germanhistorydocs.ghi-dc.org/sub_document.cfm?document_id=1548.

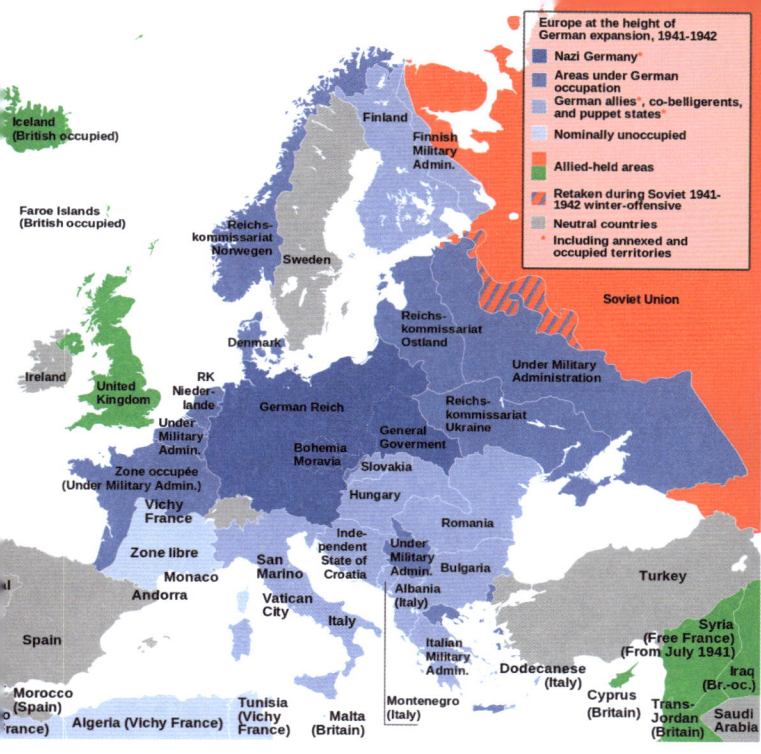

Map of Europe at the height of German control

"final solution to the Jewish Question". Post-war testimonies from Eichmann and the former Auschwitz commandant Rudolf Höss likewise claimed that it was in the late summer of 1941 that they first learned that the Jews were to be exterminated.*

Christian Gerlach, though, shifts the dating of

---

* Adolf Eichmann, 1960 and Rudolf Höss, 1946. Reproduced in Noakes & Pridham, Nazism, Vol. 3: Foreign Policy, War and Racial Extermination, pp. 1105-1106.

the decision even further forward, arguing that genocide emerged as a result of local initiatives during the autumn of 1941 and became formal policy in December. Crucial indicators here include the fact that the first experiments with Zyklon B had taken place in late September, the systematic deportation of German Jews to the east had begun in October and, by 8 December, Chelmo had been established as the first purpose-built killing centre for Jews around Lodz.

One particularly intriguing event in this process was the Wannsee Conference held just outside Berlin on 20 January 1942 to discuss the "final solution". Effectively this shows Heydrich acting on the instructions he had received the previous July. But was it here that the decision for genocide was taken, or was the conference merely convened to rubberstamp an initiative that had already been launched? Aside from Heydrich, there were no particularly high-ranking figures present for this conference; Hitler, Himmler and Göring were all absent. This in itself implies that the decision had already been taken.

Furthermore, a surviving set of minutes devotes particular attention to the treatment of the so-called Mischling Jews (people with both Jewish and "Aryan" ancestry), suggesting that the main purpose of the meeting was to work out how best to implement the regime's new policy direction, and to assert Heydrich's authority over the process. It is also worth noting that the Wannsee Conference had originally been scheduled for 9 December 1941 but had been postponed, presumably because of America's entry into the war requiring the regime's full attention. This timing would fit in with Christian Gerlach's timescale, emphasising the autumn of 1941 as the crucial decision-making period, while the fact that the meeting could be pushed back so easily to January again implies it was more about refining the details of the "final solution" than anything else.

The debate over the timing of this decision may seem rather pointless, especially when the historians concerned usually only disagree by a matter of weeks. The end result was the same, whether the policy was conceived in the summer, autumn or winter of 1941-2 or even earlier. Yet tracing the origins of this monstrous decision is crucial for our understanding of the Third Reich, and perpetrator motivation. It would, perhaps, be more convenient if all the blame for the Holocaust could be placed squarely on Hitler's shoulders. However, genocide cannot be committed by one person and this is what makes the Structuralist argument so useful. It highlights the integral role played by district leaders, police battalions, army officers, SS personnel, bureaucrats and many more who willingly helped to shape the mass murder of six million Jews. Hitler may have set the tone with his obsessive anti-semitism, but it was those beneath him who enabled him to pursue his goal of a Jew-free Europe.

Downfall

How did the Third Reich collapse?

The Nazi regime lasted 12 years before its ignoble collapse in May 1945. This time there would be none of the mythologising that had occurred at the end of the First World War; defeat was total, the Russians were in Berlin and much of the urban German landscape now lay in ruins. The party leadership were either dead, on the run or under arrest.

Some historians have expressed amazement that the Third Reich lasted as long as it did. Inherent structural problems became even more apparent during the war years as personal rivalries got in the way of essential tasks like weapons production. It took time for the German economy to mobilise fully for war and there were protracted ideological debates about the sorts of workers who should be staffing armaments factories.

Adherence to the doctrine of separate spheres and concerns for women's reproductive health meant that there was a reluctance to conscript the vast pool of female labour. The use of forced foreign labour was deemed preferable, but then various directives had to be drawn up to ensure that there was no fraternisation between these "racially inferior" workers and the "Aryan" population. The military effort, overseen by Hitler as commander-in-chief, was also beset by strategic blunders, most notably the over-extension into the Soviet Union.

Indeed, the war had been going badly for the Germans since the battle of Stalingrad, a protracted fight that lasted from August 1942 until February 1943 and left an estimated two million men dead or wounded. Defeat had been brought about by a number of factors: the Germans were ill-equipped to deal with the harsh winter, lacking food, fuel and adequate clothing. Frostbite was common. It became a war of attrition and, even when the army did make advances in the city, they failed to capitalise on them or hold on to the new territory for long. Soon, ammunition was running short, too.

The fact that the city was named after Stalin fuelled the Soviet campaign to hang on to it, while also ensuring that Hitler remained steadfast in his determination to capture it; both sides recognised the propaganda potential of winning this particular battle.

Consequently, Hitler ignored requests from his commanders in the field to organise a tactical retreat, ordering them to fight on whatever the cost. Unfortunately for the Germans, this ultimately resulted in a massive loss of manpower and they did not win any further decisive battles on the eastern front.

The Red Army, on the other hand, were given a fresh confidence and proceeded with their march westwards, pushing the Wehrmacht back towards Germany. By June 1944, the country was facing a two-front war as the western Allies landed in Normandy and began their own advance; German forces were now stretched beyond measure and defeat was inevitable.

Stalingrad had a serious impact on public morale, particularly since the official narrative up to now had been stressing the invincibility of the German fighting machine. The *Sicherheitsdienst* (Security Service – SD) reported a rise in the number of anti-Hitler jokes in circulation and the regime was forced to withdraw its "Hitler is victory" poster from public display. Allied strategic bombing of German cities was also taking its toll, leaving thousands dead or homeless: 42,600 people died during the fire bombing of Hamburg alone in 1943, while a similar attack on Dresden in 1945 killed an estimated 25,000. The aerial bombardment damaged vital road and rail networks and utilities, and disrupted food supplies. Day-to-day life, which had previously retained some sense of normality, became more and more difficult.

Yet, despite these challenges, the German people continued to fight on to the bitter end. University students and then teenage Hitler Youth members were drafted into the military effort and in September 1944 the regime established the *Volkssturm* (People's Storm), a motley crew assembled from all remaining civilian men. The group lacked basic equipment and training but were expected to join in the battle to ward off the advancing Red Army. Thousands were killed in the process but still the Germans pushed on.

To some extent, this determination might be regarded as proof of the final success of Nazi propaganda and the whole concept of *Volksgemeinschaft*. Certainly, Goebbels's "total war" speech on 18 February 1943 had played upon this rhetoric and exhorted people to follow the Führer's lead and work as hard as possible to secure victory. A loss of morale had been routinely held up as the explanation for Germany's defeat in the First World War and the Nazis were desperate to ensure there would be no repeat of this.

A combination of patriotism and fear, however, were the more likely driving forces. Whatever people may have come to think about Nazism, there was a fervent desire to defend the country and, after years of anti-Bolshevist propaganda, a very real sense of terror about would happen if Germany should fall into Soviet hands. The Red Army, though, was not the only institution inducing fear. The Nazi regime itself had been cracking down on the slightest sign of dissent ever since the failed July bomb plot of 1944.

A massive investigation had been launched to root out all of those linked to the main conspirators, while the notorious *Volksgericht* (People's Court) was increasingly wielding the death penalty for the slightest offence. In this climate, anyone caught uttering defeatist comments or failing to throw their weight behind the war effort was liable to be shot. Ironically, as the German military front was collapsing, the Nazis were continuing to tighten their grip over the home front with more and more power taken out of state institutions and given to the SS and the party.

Ultimately, nothing could halt the Allied advance. During the final weeks of the Third Reich, several high-profile members of the Nazi leadership including Heinrich Himmler began to slink away and unilaterally open negotiations for a surrender. An enraged Hitler expelled them from the party but, by the end of April, he too was forced to concede that everything was lost as the Red Army descended on the capital. On 30 April 1945, Adolf Hitler committed suicide in his Berlin bunker. Days later, his named successor, Grand Admiral Karl Dönitz, surrendered to the Allies. The Third Reich had fallen.

GLOSSARY OF KEY TERMS, INSTITUTIONS AND ABBREVIATIONS

Anschluss union of Germany and Austria; banned under the 1919 Treaty of Versailles.

Aryan racial grouping used to denote the supposed "master race" of northern Europe that was generally perceived as having blonde hair and blue eyes.

BDM the German Girls League; female equivalent of the Hitler Youth.

DAF the German Labour Front; a Nazi organisation to represent the workers and which replaced traditional trade unions in 1933.

Einsatzgruppen mobile killing squads that shot thousands of civilians following the invasion of the Soviet Union in 1941.

"Final Solution" Nazi euphemism to describe the endpoint of their persecution of the Jews and taken to refer directly to physical extermination.

Freikorps a right-wing paramilitary organisation made up of ex-servicemen and nationalists that engaged in public acts of violence during the Weimar Republic.

Gestapo the secret police.

Gleichschaltung the coordination of German politics and society under Nazism; used to describe Hitler's consolidation of power, 1933-1934.

Intentionalism a school of thought that emphasises the role of Hitler in decision-making, views the Third Reich as a totalitarian regime and suggests that the Nazis had a clear programme for implementing their goals.

Kaiserreich term used to describe the German empire that ruled from 1871-1918.

KPD the German Communist Party.

Kristallnacht "the night of broken glass" – nationwide pogrom against the Jews on 9 November 1938.

Lebensraum living space; the acquisition of land to sustain Germany's growing population.

Mittelstand term for the traditional middle class.

November Criminals derogatory term used to describe the politicians who signed the Armistice at the end of the First World War.

NSDAP the National Socialist German Workers' Party (commonly known as the Nazi Party).

Operation Barbarossa codename for the invasion of the Soviet Union in June 1941.

Pogrom a mass riot or act of violence targeted against a particular ethnic group and most commonly associated with the persecution of Jews.

Reichstag the main chamber of the German parliament.

SA Nazi paramilitary organisation known as stormtroopers.

SOPADE the Social Democratic Party in Exile which compiled reports on German public opinion during the Third Reich.

SPD the left-wing Social Democratic Party that played a leading role in the government of the Weimar Republic and was a source of opposition to the Nazis.

SS security squad that controlled the police system and concentration camps.

"stab in the back" the mythology that Germany's defeat in World War One was the result of morale being undermined by left-wing politicians, black marketeers and Jews.

Structuralism school of historical thought that holds that the Third Reich was an inherently confused and unstable regime where decisions emerged almost by accident and Hitler was a weak dictator.

Volksgemeinschaft the Nazis' utopian vision of society or "People's Community" based on race.

Völkisch nationalism an aggressive form of nationalism based on race.

Waffen-SS military arm of the SS.

Wehrmacht term denoting the German armed forces.

Weimar city near Leipzig where the democratic constitution of the German republic was drawn up after the First World War: hence the Weimar Republic.

A SHORT CHRONOLOGY

1918
3-9 November: naval mutinies and the formation of workers' and soldiers' councils.
9 November: proclamation of the Weimar Republic.
11 November: signing of the Armistice.

1919
5-11 January: Spartacist uprising.
9 January: Anton Drexler founds the German Workers' Party in Munich.
19 January: election of the National Assembly; Friedrich Ebert becomes the first President of the Weimar Republic.
28 June: signing of the Treaty of Versailles.

1920
24 February: the German Workers' Party is renamed the National Socialist German Workers' Party (NSDAP) and the 25 point party programme is published.

1921
29 July: Adolf Hitler assumes leadership of the NSDAP.

1923
11 January: French troops occupy the Ruhr.
8-9 November: Hitler launches his Munich Putsch.

1924
26 February: Hitler goes on trial for high treason.
1 April: Hitler sentenced to five years' imprisonment.
20 December: Hitler is released.

1925
27 February: the NSDAP is re-established.
25 April: Paul von Hindenburg becomes President of the Weimar Republic.

1929
24 October: Wall Street Crash.

1930
30 March: Heinrich Brüning becomes chancellor and institutes an array of spending cuts.
14 September: the NSDAP makes its national breakthrough, winning 107 seats in the Reichstag elections.

1932
10 April: Hindenburg defeats Hitler to be re-elected as German President.
13 April: Brüning bans the SA after a spate of public violence.
1 June: Franz von Papen becomes the new German chancellor.
14 June: the ban on the SA is lifted, prompting violence to resume.
31 July: the NSDAP becomes the biggest party in the Reichstag, winning 230 seats in the latest elections. Hindenburg refuses Hitler's demand to be made chancellor.
6 November: further Reichstag elections see a decline in the NSDAP vote but they remain the biggest single party.
4 December: Kurt von Schleicher replaces von Papen as chancellor.

1933
30 January: Hitler replaces Schleicher as chancellor.

27 February: Reichstag fire.
5 March: final Reichstag elections give the NSDAP 44 per cent of the vote.
21 March: Day of Potsdam.
22 March: first concentration camp opened at Dachau.
24 March: passing of the Enabling Act.
1 April: one day boycott of Jewish businesses.
7 April: "Law for the Restoration of the Professional Civil Service" removes Jews from public office.
2 May: trade unions are abolished.
14 July: other political parties are banned; "Law for the Prevention of Hereditarily Diseased Offspring" allows for forced sterilisation of people considered racially "undesirable".

1934
30 June: Night of the Long Knives purges members of the SA.
1-2 August: death of President Hindenburg; Hitler becomes supreme ruler of Germany.

1935
16 March: reintroduction of conscription.
15 September: introduction of the Nuremberg Laws, depriving Jews of German citizenship.

1936
7-28 March: remilitarisation of the Rhineland.
1 August: Berlin Olympics begin.
19 October: Hitler announces the start of the Four Year Plan to prepare Germany for war.

1937
5 November: Hossbach Memorandum records Hitler's thoughts on the possible format of a future war.

1938
11 March: Anschluss with Austria.
15-30 September: Hitler meets with Chamberlain and eventually succeeds in acquiring the Sudetenland.
9 November: Kristallnacht pogrom.
12 November: "Decree for the Exclusion of Jews from German Economic Life" enables Germans to take over Jewish businesses.

1939
15-16 March: invasion of the rest of Czechoslovakia.
21 March: Hitler demands the return of Danzig.
23 August: signing of the Nazi-Soviet Pact.
1 September: invasion of Poland.
3 September: Britain and France declare war on Germany.
October: beginning of the "euthanasia" programme against disabled people.

1940
9 April: invasion of Norway and Denmark.
14 May: the Netherlands are captured.
28 May: Belgium is captured.
22 June: armistice signed between Germany and France.

1941
6 April: invasion of Yugoslavia.
22 June: invasion of the Soviet Union.
31 July: Reinhard Heydrich ordered to prepare for the "Final Solution of the Jewish Question".
28-29 Sept: 34,000 Jews murdered at Babi-Yar near Kiev.
8 December: Chelmno established as a killing centre.
11 December: Germany declares war on the USA.

1942
20 January: Wannsee Conference.

1 March: gassings begin at Belzec extermination camp.
30 March: First transport of Jews from Western Europe arrives in Auschwitz.

1943
2 February: Battle of Stalingrad ends in defeat.
18 February: Joseph Goebbels issues his "total war" speech.

1944
20 July: failure of the bomb plot against Hitler.

1945
30 April: Hitler commits suicide.
7 May: Germany surrenders.

FURTHER READING

Richard Bessel, *Life in the Third Reich* (Oxford: Oxford University Press, 1987).

Michael Burleigh & Wolfgang Wippermann, *The Racial State: Germany, 1933-1945* (Cambridge: Cambridge University Press, 1991).

Thomas Childers & Jane Caplan (eds), *Re-Evaluating the Third Reich* (New York: Holmes & Meier, 1993).

David Crew, *Nazism and German Society, 1933-45* (London: Routledge, 1994).

Matthew Hughes & Chris Mann, *Inside Hitler's Germany: Life under the Third Reich* (London: Brassey's, 2002).

Ian Kershaw, *The Nazi Dictatorship: Problems and Perspectives of Interpretation* (London: Bloomsbury, 1993).

Hans Mommsen (ed.), *The Third Reich Between Vision and Reality* (Oxford: Berg, 2002).

Detlev Peukert, *Inside Nazi Germany: Conformity, Opposition and Racism in Everyday Life* (London: Penguin, 1993).

Matthew Seligman, *In the Shadow of the Swastika Life in Germany under the Nazis, 1933-1945* (Staplehurst: Spellmount, 2003).

William Shirer, *The Rise and Fall of the Third Reich: A History of Nazi Germany* (London: Simon & Schuster, anniversary edition 2011).

INDEX

A
Adenuaer, Konrad 78
Allied forces
    World War I 9, 10, 11–15, 19
    World War II 58, 88–92, 94, 111–112
Amann, Max 51
Animal welfare 62
Anschluss (union), with Austria 88, 155
anti-Semitism 24–25, 27–28, 34–35, 81, 83, 95–96, 102
Armistice (1918) 9, 21
Art, policies on 27, 50, 57
Article 48, Weimar Constitution 18–19, 35, 43–44
"Aryan" race 26, 38, 60, 83–84, 86, 108, 110
Austria 25, 27, 28, 88, 97, 103, 155
Authoritarianism 14, 16

B
Belgium 30, 93
Berlin Olympics 56, 94, 120
Bessel, Richard 17
Bolshevism 17–18, 35, 39, 104, 113
Book burning 50, 56
Bracher, Karl-Dietrich 8, 52
Braun, Eva 29
Britain 13–14, 88–89, 91–92
Brockdorff-Rantzau, Count 11–12
Broszat, Martin 8, 52, 104
Browning, Christopher 7, 106

C
Capitalism 24, 39
Censorship 27, 50
Chamberlain, Neville 88
Chanel, Coco 64
Church 38–39, 41, 80–81
Churchill, Winston 64
Classes, social 4, 6, 14, 18, 26, 36, 39–40, 80

Colonies 11, 15, 105
Communism 38, 40, 46, 78, 79, 91
Communists 43, 46, 85
Concentration camps 46–47, 60, 84, 94, 96–97
Czechoslovakia 59–60, 88, 103

D
Dachau concentration camp 46–47, 97, 98
Danzig crisis (1939) 89–90
Democracy, Parliamentary 4, 16–17, 18–19, 20, 27, 32, 39
Disabled people 63, 71, 80
Dönitz, Karl 114
Dresden bombings 112
Drexler, Anton 24
Drug use 64

E
Eastern Europe 59, 60–61, 89, 90, 93, 108
Ebert, Friedrich 18, 20
Eichmann, Adolf 6, 105, 107
Einsatzgruppen (mobile killings squads) 59, 61, 103, 106
Eisenhower, Dwight D. 64
Elser, Georg 79–80
Enabling Act (1933) 44–45, 49
Europe, occupation of 93, *107*
Evans, Richard 5
Extermination camps 60, 61, 98, 103, 108

F
Fascism 4, 23
Four Year Plan 50–51, 57, 88, 91
France 13, 30, 88–89, 93
Freikorps (paramilitary group) 18, 115

G
Gellately, Robert 85–86

Genocide *see* Holocaust
Gerlach, Christian 107–109
Gerlich, Fritz 23
German Empire (*Kaiserreich*) 6–7, 14–15
German Labour Front (DAF) 51, 67–68, 115
German unification (1871) 6, 14, 16
German Workers' Party 24
Germany
  economic crisis 16, 19–20, 30, 33–34, 37, 39–40
  economic recovery 65–67, 68, 110
  "golden years" (1924-1928) 22
  history pre-WWI 6–7, 14–15
  impact of WWI 7, 9–15, 19–21, 24, 25, 30, 33
  post-WWII 78
  social revolution (1918-1919) 17–18
  see also Third Reich; Weimar Republic
Gestapo 50, 57, 59, 60, 63, 79–80, 84–86, 99
Ghettos 62, 103, 105
Goebbels, Joseph *13*, 32, 45–46, 56–57, 71, 100, 113
Goldhagen, Daniel 7, 95, 100
Göring, Hermann 36, 50–51, 57–58, 88
Great Depression 16, 33, 40

H
Hamburg 40, 112
Hess, Rudolf 58–59
Heydrich, Reinhard 59–60, 100, 106, 108
Hillgruber, Andreas 52, 90
Himmler, Heinrich *45*, 59, 60–61, *61*, 84, 114
Hindenburg, Paul von 29, 35, 36, 42, 47, 49
Hitler, Adolf 4–5, 7–8
  anti-Semitism 28, 103–104, 109
  as artist 28
  assassination attempts 79–80, 82–83
  belief in Social Darwinism 28, 51–52, 53
  biography in brief 28–29
  as Chancellor 15, 16, 29, 30, 35–37, 42–49
  consolidation of power 42–49, 115
  "Cult of the Führer" 33–34, 56, 66–68
  as dictator, weak *vs.* total 7, 52–55
  downfall 111–112
  early imprisonment 31–32
  electoral support for 37–41, *41*
  in German Workers' Party 24, 29
  images of *13*, *28*, *33*, *45*, *87*
  resistance to 77–85
  response to Versailles Treaty 12, 15
  rise to power 19, 24, 28, 30–37
  suicide 29, 56, 114
  vegetarianism 62
  in World War I 28
  works:
    Mein Kampf 32, 86, 89–90
    Zweites Buch ("Second Book") 89–90
Hitler Youth 21–22, 74–76, 81–82, 93, 112
Hofer, Walter 79
Holocaust 4–5, 7, 53–54, 59, 60, 63–64, 95
  "Final solution" 59–60, 102–109
Holy Roman Empire 6, 62
Höppner, Rolf-Heinz 105
Hossbach Memorandum (1937) 92, 120

I
Intentionalism 8, 52–55, 89–92, 104, 116
Israel, war crimes trials 6
Italy 14, 30–31

J
Jäckel, Eberhard 8, 52
Jehovah's Witnesses 85, 97
Jews

anti-Semitism 24–25, 27–28, 34–35, 81, 83, 95–96, 102
blame for WWI 10, 21
deaths 63
discrimination against 65, 67, 77, 98–100, 103
extermination camps 60, 61, 98, 103, 108
Kristallnacht ("night of broken glass") 59, 100–102
Nuremberg Laws (1935) 58, 67, 98–99, 103
responses to prosecution, Germans' 94–102
support for 62, 82, 100–101
see also Holocaust
July Bomb Plot (1944) 82–83, 113

K

KdF ("Strength Through Joy") programme 68–70
Kershaw, Ian 8, 54–55, 78–79, 96, 100–101
Kessler, Count Henry 20
KPD (German communist party) 33, 38, 40, 43, 44, 78, 79, 85
Kristallnacht ("night of broken glass") 59, 100–102

L

Lazowski, Eugene 62
League of Nations 13, 22
Lebensraum (living space), expansionist policy 25, 86, 90, 93, 116
Liebknecht, Karl 17–18
Luftwaffe (air force) 11, 57, 58, 72
Luxembourg, Rosa 17–18

M

Mann, Thomas 23
Maschmann, Melita 101
Minority groups 27, 77, 85, 86, 97
Moeller van den Bruck, Arthur 62
Mommsen, Hans 8, 50, 52, 53, 78, 104
Müller, Heinrich 63

Munich Conference 88
Munich Putsch (1923) 30–31, 57, 58, 60
Mussolini, Benito 30–31

N

National Socialism 4–5
ideologies of 4–5, 23–29, 67, 75–77, 113
popular support for 5–7, 37–38, 78
rise after WWI 12–13
Nazi Party
'25 Points' programme 24–27, 86
domestic policy 65–77, *73*
early years 12, 16, 22, 23
electoral support for 37–41, *41*
Enabling Act (1933) 44–45, 49
foreign policy 4, 68, 86–93
health and lifestyle 62, 63
leaders of 36, 56–61, 62, 114
move to dictatorship 42–49
propaganda 10, 16, 26, 28, 33–35, 38, 48–50, 56, 113
racism of 4–5, 25–26, 28, 75, 83, 84, 86, 93–109
rise to power 30–37
Swastika symbol 63
Netherlands, invasion of 93
"Night of the Long Knives" 47–48, 60, 67
Noakes, Jeremy 51
NSDAP (National Socialist German Workers' Party) *see* Nazi Party
Nuremberg Laws (1935) 58, 98–99
Nuremberg trials 5, 6, 58–59, 89, 92, 107

P

Poland 38–39, 63, 83, 93, 103, 105
extermination camps in 4, 98, 108
invasion of 54, 88–89, 91
Political opponents 43–44, 46–47, 65, 97, 113
Potsdam, Day of 48–49
Prussia 11, 36, 37, 57

R

Racism 4–5, 25–26, 28, 75, 83, 84, 86, 93–109
Rallies and parades 28, 34, 49, 56
Reich Labour Service 66, 93
Reichstag (German parliament) 44–46, 48, 57
  fire 42–43
Reparations for WWI 11–13, 19–20, 30, 33
Resistance movements 76, 77–85
Ribbentrop, Joachim von 90–91
Rich, Norman 50, 52
Röhm, Ernst 47–48

S

SA (paramilitary group; stormtroopers) 21–22, 35, 39, 44, 46–48, 50, 98, 100
Scheidemann, Philipp 12, 15
Scholl, Hans and Sophie 82
SD (*Sicherheitsdienst*, Security Service) 59, 112
Slavs 93, 95–96
Social Darwinism 28, 51–52, 53
Social Democratic Party (SPD) 14–15, 17, 38, 39–40, 45, 79, 117
Socialism 14–15, 17
Soviet Union 63, 89–91, 103, 106, 111, 113–114
Spartacist Uprising (1919) 17–18
SS (Security Squadron) 47–50, 59, 60, 61, 67, 84–85, 114
Stalingrad, battle of 67, 111–112
Stauffenberg, Claus von 82–83
Structuralism 8, 52–55, 91–92, 104–106, 109, 117
Swastika symbol 63
Swing Youth 76, 82

T

Taylor, A.J.P. 92
Third Reich 4–5, 7–8
  chronology 118–122
  collapse 110–114
  establishment 42–49
  everyday Germans in 5–7, 94–102
  name origins 7, 62
  ten facts about 62–64
  terror state 84–86
  see also National Socialism; Nazi Party
Totalitarianism 8, 27
Trade unions 39, 47, 67, 85

U

United Kingdom 13–14, 88–89, 91–92
United States 9, 13, 16, 20, 33, 109

V

Van der Lubbe, Marinus 43
Versailles, Treaty of 10–15, 19–21, 25, 68, 86, 93
Völkisch (ethno-) nationalism 24, 27
Volksgemeinschaft ("People's Community") ideology 26–27, 67, 75–77, 113
Volkssturm ("People's Storm") 61, 112

W

Wall Street Crash (1929) 16, 20, 33
Wannsee Conference (1942) 60, 108–109
Weidemann, Fritz 53
Weimar Republic 15–23, 27, 29–32, 35–36, 42–43
Wilhelm I of Prussia 6, 14
Wilhelm II, Kaiser 7, *14*, 14–16
Willikens, Werner 55
Wilson, Woodrow 13
Women 6, 22, 65–66, 70–72, *73*, 77, 110
World War I 7, 9–15, 19–21, 24, 25, 28, 113
World War II 4–5, 57–58, 61, 68
  end 110–112
  outbreak 88–89, 91, 93, 103

Y

Young people 40–41, 72–76, *73*, 81–82, 98

First published in 2016 by
Connell Guides
Artist House
35 Little Russell Street
London WC1A 2HH

10 9 8 7 6 5 4 3 2 1

Copyright © Connell Guides Publishing Ltd.
All rights reserved. No part of this publication
may be reproduced, stored in a retrieval system or transmitted in any
form, or by any means (electronic, mechanical, or otherwise) without
the prior written permission of both the copyright owners
and the publisher.

Picture credits:
p.13 © Bettmann/ Getty Images
p.33 © The LIFE Picture Collection / Getty Images
p.45 © AFP / Stringer / Getty Images
p.73 © Bettmann/ Getty Images
p.87 © Bettmann/ Getty Images

A CIP catalogue record for this book is available from the British Library.
ISBN 978-1-911187-52-3

Design © Nathan Burton

Assistant Editor and typeset by:
Paul Woodward

Printed in Great Britain by
Bell and Bain Ltd, Glasgow

www.connellguides.com